If you're a doubter, we  make you laugh, make you c_____ ___s authenticity is not only _____g; it's enlightening.

MARK BATTERSON, *New York Times* bestselling author of *The Circle Maker*, lead pastor of National Community Church

Most Christians think evangelism is about trying to convince nonbelievers to believe what Christians believe. In Western culture, this is painfully awkward and rarely effective, which is why, despite the New Testament's many instructions to spread the Good News, most Christians understandably shy away from it. In *The Doubters' Club*, Preston Ulmer uses compelling stories, insightful biblical teaching, and a healthy dose of refreshingly raw (and, often, comically self-deprecating) honesty to lay out a radically different and much more compelling model of evangelism. Among other things, instead of trying to rescue skeptics from their doubts, Ulmer encourages Christians to simply befriend skeptics *as they are*, which includes affirming and exploring their doubts. Perhaps most importantly, Ulmer is one of those gifted communicators who *inspires* readers at least as much as he informs them. *The Doubters' Club* stirred a fire in me for evangelism that I confess had become rather cool over time. I am confident this book will have a similar effect on most who read it with an open mind, which is why I sincerely hope *The Doubters' Club* finds its way into the hands of a great multitude of Christians.

GREG BOYD, senior pastor of Woodland Hills Church, president of ReKnew.org, author of *Benefit of the Doubt*

The Doubters' Club comes at just the right time. We live in a time of political, racial, and ideological division. This book helps us see the image of God in all people, love them for who they are, and listen and lift them up from wherever they are.

WALTER HARVEY, president of the National Black Fellowship

I love both the evangelism and discipleship that is taking place through the Doubters' Club! Preston makes it possible for any of us to live with Christlike love without having to have all the answers. This book is a true north for anyone who wants to have meaningful relationships with doubters and skeptics.

DOUG CLAY, general superintendent of The Assemblies of God

This book is for the cynics, dreamers, hesitant hopefuls, and the ones all too familiar with being shamed for their doubting. Preston Ulmer shares how to move past motivations of evangelical spiritual-trophy collections to genuinely seeing and loving others authentically and naturally. *The Doubters' Club* is simply a stunning display of God's desire to know and love us. Are you doubting? Are you in need of a fresh perspective on how to love others as they are? Are you hopeful for unity in relationships that seem to get stuck over arguments and petty disagreements? This book is for you.

CANDACE PAYNE (CHEWBACCA MOM), author, speaker, viral sensation

Preston is a practitioner of what is presented in *The Doubters' Club*. His writing stirs my confidence that in an increasingly skeptical world, the gospel is and always will be good news for the curious and not-yet-convinced. Preston solidifies the truth that guided wrestling with faith questions, concerns, and doubts does not have to cause someone to drift away from Christ—in fact, it might cause them to drift toward him. I highly recommend this book!

JEFFERY PORTMANN, director of the Church Multiplication Network

I have been inspired by the life and ministry of Preston Ulmer for years now, and I am so thankful that he is putting the brilliance of the Doubters' Club into book form. This resource will not only help doubters find faith in Christ but also help Christians to create healthy environments for doubters to wrestle with their beliefs. This book will help the church truly be the church. I highly recommend this book and look forward to the lives that will be transformed because of it.

DR. AARON BURKE, pastor of Radiant Church

The Doubters' Club exists for the curious at heart. It forms a bridge that can connect people with different worldviews in a safe and honoring space. It is a comforting reminder that we are more than allowed to ask questions.

HOLLYN, American singer and songwriter

Preston Ulmer officially joins the ranks of historic Christian writers such as C. S. Lewis, Mother Teresa, Martin Luther, and Charles Spurgeon, all of whom in like manner laid bare their own doubter's souls. It takes audacity to display your uncertainties, but Preston Ulmer sees the future and how evangelism will play out in the days ahead. Through masterful storytelling and a strong dose of academic rigor, Preston dispels the myth that our doubts need to remain secret and undisclosed. Instead, *The Doubters' Club* will show you how to leverage your doubts toward a life of conviction and influence.

DR. SCOTT HAGAN, author, president of North Central University

The Doubters' Club welcomes people across dividing lines to explore genuine conversations about life, faith, and purpose. Read this book with your friends, and join the conversation!

DR. DAVID DOCUSEN, author of *Neighborliness: Finding the Beauty of God across Dividing Lines*

GOOD-FAITH CONVERSATIONS
WITH SKEPTICS, ATHEISTS,
AND THE SPIRITUALLY
WOUNDED

THE
Doubters'
CLUB

THE
Doubters'
CLUB

THE
Doubters'
CLUB

PRESTON ULMER

A NavPress resource published in alliance
with Tyndale House Publishers

NavPress is the publishing ministry of The Navigators, an international Christian organization and leader in personal spiritual development. NavPress is committed to helping people grow spiritually and enjoy lives of meaning and hope through personal and group resources that are biblically rooted, culturally relevant, and highly practical.

For more information, visit NavPress.com.

The Doubters' Club: Good-Faith Conversations with Skeptics, Atheists, and the Spiritually Wounded

Copyright © 2021 by Preston Ulmer. All rights reserved.

A NavPress resource published in alliance with Tyndale House Publishers

NavPress and the NavPress logo are registered trademarks of NavPress, The Navigators, Colorado Springs, CO. *Tyndale* is a registered trademark of Tyndale House Ministries. Absence of ® in connection with marks of NavPress or other parties does not indicate an absence of registration of those marks.

The Team:
David Zimmerman, Acquisitions Editor; Elizabeth Schroll, Copy Editor; Olivia Eldredge, Operations Manager; Julie Chen, Designer

Cover photograph of stacked mugs by Samantha Ram on Unsplash.

Author photo taken by Megan White, copyright © 2021. All rights reserved.

The author is represented by the literary agency of WordServe Literary, www.wordserveliterary.com.

Some of the anecdotal illustrations in this book are true to life and are included with the permission of the persons involved. All other illustrations are composites of real situations, and any resemblance to people living or dead is purely coincidental.

For information about special discounts for bulk purchases, please contact Tyndale House Publishers at csresponse@tyndale.com, or call 1-855-277-9400.

ISBN 978-1-64158-335-0

Printed in the United States of America

27	26	25	24	23	22	21
7	6	5	4	3	2	1

For my wife, Lisa.

You believed in me when I didn't believe in God.

The one thing I have never doubted is your love for me.

CONTENTS

INTRODUCTION

Great Minds Do Not Think Alike

> *Whether the questions are old or new—or angry varieties of*
> *either—we should be more engaging and less confrontational*
> *in our sharing of the good news. We must find new hinges*
> *upon which to swing open new doors.*
> RANDY NEWMAN, *Questioning Evangelism*

IN 1618, playwright Dabridgcourt Belchier expressed an idea that has outlived the ancient English of its time: "Good wits doe jumpe,"[1] by which he meant what has become a cliché: "Great minds think alike." Since then, we have been playfully commending one another for sharing our thoughts and our opinions. I would dare say that celebrating the person who thinks and believes like us is far older than the seventeenth century.

The ironic part of it all is that every one of us thinks we are right.

When I was in seminary, I heard a quote that shared a similar idea. With conviction, my professor would often quote a famous philosopher by saying: "What monstrosities would walk the streets were some people's faces as unfinished as their minds?"[2] The quote is a profound way of saying, "If you aren't certain about everything you believe, you're a monster."

After two master's degrees, years of pastoral ministry, and years of being an Uber driver, I couldn't disagree more. People who think about the complexities of life and are perplexed by belief in God are not "monsters." Most people approach those who think differently than them with anxiety, frustration, and resistance. Dismissive of their views. Discouraged by their lack of faith. We have been trained by the cultural cliché that "great minds think alike." We use this sort of rhetoric when it comes to categories like sports and our favorite restaurants . . . and we apply it by refusing to genuinely connect with the person we are inwardly condemning—mostly because connection and condemnation can't share the same space.

In every society there have always been people who are committed to connection in spite of differences. Poets, artists, and TED Talks teach us that great minds do not think alike! The people of the ancient Near East saw the mind as the seat of the emotions. It was, what we call in American culture, the heart. Great hearts feel differently. They process, think, remember, bleed, and heal in a multitude of ways. Jesus never calls those unlike him monsters for their unbelief. He brought unbelievers and religious Pharisees together to help them move toward the Father. Together.

His tactics were different than ours. Jesus had a way of

making the supposed "monsters" look beautiful. Few people have written about this as accurately as Flannery O' Connor. In her short story "Revelation," Ruby Turpin is a legalistic woman likened to a bigot of the worse kind. Amid her self-righteous posture is her unrelenting judgment toward those who need even the slightest dose of conventional grace. As the story develops, however, her final epiphany is an emotionally hazardous one. She has a mystical vision of bridges and pathways to heaven. Reuniting the saved and the damned, O' Connor writes:

> A visionary light settled in her eyes. She saw the streak as a vast swinging bridge extending upward from the earth through a field of living fire. Upon it a vast horde of souls were rumbling toward heaven . . . [along with] battalions of freaks and lunatics shouting and clapping and leaping like frogs. . . . She recognized at once . . . those who, like herself and Claud, had always had a little of everything and the God-given wit to use it right. . . . Yet she could see by their shocked and altered faces that even their virtues were being burned away.[3]

What a satirical representation of Jesus' heart. The freaks and lunatics are the most desperate to become the free and lovely. They are more eager to get in. "Even the prostitutes and tax collectors will enter the Kingdom before you" (Matthew 21:31, author's paraphrase). Jesus had a way of holding ground for those who would be considered doubters and skeptics.

He was persuasive, not argumentative.

Curious, not critical.

Careful, not crushing.

Asked, but didn't assume.

Connected before he corrected.

Jesus was not the loudest proclaimer of what he believed to be true, but he was the busiest doer of what he knew to be love.

This is the driving force of the book. Whom Jesus loved, how Jesus loved them, and why it is still the most effective way to make disciples. My atheist friend, Sam, said it best: "The Christians who come to the Doubters' Clubs aren't Christians. They are Jesus people." I'm proud to admit we look more like freaks and lunatics than we do Mrs. Turpins.

The Doubters' Club was birthed when I asked an atheist coffee-shop owner what type of church he would go to. You can try to be as winsome as possible, but some questions are just bizarre. This was one of those questions. Taken off guard, he responded with, "I don't go to church. I'm an atheist."

"Oh, I used to not believe in all this either!" I genuinely felt a connection. "But if you *did* go to church, what type of church would you go to?"

I wasn't interested in converting him. My family would be moving to Denver soon to start a fresh expression of Jesus, and I had no idea where to start. I was merely asking a local for advice.

"Okay . . . *if* I went to church, I would go somewhere where I could ask questions and I wasn't judged for thinking differently."

What an incredible answer! My new friend would go somewhere as long as he was able to think for himself. Months later, we started the Doubters' Club together. Doubters' Clubs are gatherings led by a Christian and a non-Christian who model friendship and pursue truth together. It is not an apologetics ministry. It is a club for the "monsters." Great minds don't think alike at the Doubters' Club.

This book is not my plan for franchising the Doubters' Club. I realize it's not for everyone. The purpose of the next nine chapters is to show that the Doubters' Club isn't a new thing to do. It's a new way to do everything. It is a lifestyle that builds bridges where there used to be barriers and sets us free from "closing the deal" every time we converse with people who do not think like us. In fact, making disciples isn't getting people to think like us at all. Thinking like us may be the barrier, not the bridge.

My prayer is that each chapter is a grace of God to you. A means of renewing your mind. To borrow a phrase from my friend Greg Boyd: "Rethink everything you thought you knew."[4] I have a hunch that current practices of evangelism leave you feeling frustrated and defeated, and I am confident that they are off-putting to our unbelieving brothers and sisters. Fixing these practices is certainly killing us. I'm writing this with nonbelievers in mind. So, for the sake of their salvation and your freedom, would you accept my invitation into the Doubters' Club? If you already have objections and questions about some of the things I have said—perfect! That means we don't think like one another, and it's going to be a great meeting. Grab a drink.

Let's pursue truth together, my friend.

1

GOD OF THE DOUBTER

Out of the Faith, into the Kingdom

*Loss is like a wind, it either carries you to a new destination
or it traps you in an ocean of stagnation. You must quickly
learn how to navigate the sail, for stagnation is death.*

VAL UCHENDU

So, you're telling me there's a chance?

LLOYD CHRISTMAS, *Dumb and Dumber*

THE FIRST TIME I SAW *DUMB AND DUMBER*, I was reduced to a dribbling, hysterical wreck. I don't remember the where, when, or who I was with, but I can recall most of the lines. I learned that "you can't triple stamp a double stamp," and there is no use in arguing over it. I also learned that traveling four inches, according to the map, is incredibly disappointing on a road trip. Jim Carey and Jeff Daniels had a way of tossing my intellectual pretensions out the window for an hour and forty-seven minutes and filling my brain with laugh-worthy quotes. Among all the lines, there is an iconic scene between Jim Carey's character, Lloyd Christmas, and his love interest, Mary Swanson. It has since become a classic moment in American cinematography.

Lloyd finds that he is in love with Mary, who is part of a scheme that he is trying to rescue her from. In one moment, they are alone together, and he says to her:

"What do you think the chances are of a guy like you and a girl like me . . . ending up together?" . . .

"Not good," she says.

Lloyd persists. "You mean . . . not good like one out of a hundred?"

She says, "I'd say more like one out of a million."

After a long pause Lloyd's countenance is lifted as he sees the silver lining in it all. With newfound confidence he says that classic line: "So, you're telling me there's a chance?"

If you have ever known someone who was once a Christian but has since become a skeptic or doubter, it can often feel like Lloyd had a better chance at taking Mary out than they have at returning to Jesus. They have just enough questions to sink the ship they used to sail and just enough Bible knowledge to poke holes in yours. Honestly, it can be a frightening thing. These people are famously identified as "nones." No affiliation with religious beliefs or practices. In October of 2020, there was a post on the *Religion in Public* blog by Professors Paul Djupe and Ryan Burge. As they continue to research the decline of religion, they stated that "the most momentous change in American religion over the last

25 years has been the growth of the religious nones from 5 percent in 1994 to 34 percent in 2019."[1]

Author John S. Dickerson saw a growing number of nones back in 2013. According to Dickerson's book *The Great Evangelical Recession*, reports were showing an increase in the amount of people who would not consider themselves religious. And an even larger number of people than ever who are abandoning the faith.

"The natural, fear-based reaction to these changes," Dickerson writes, "is to raise our guard and fight for our rights."[2] Based on the statistics, it's safe to say fear-based reactions are not winning others over. It's time we respond, not react.

Most of us are connected to someone who falls into one of these statistics: the not religious or the ones who have abandoned the faith altogether. Please do not lose heart! Believe it or not, stepping away from a faith that they do not sincerely hold to is the right move to make. I was once a spiritual seeker, doubter, and abandoner of the faith. Let me tell you what drew me back into the Christian faith.

It was a person, not a program.

A detour, not a destination.

A commitment, not a conversion.

A patience, not a prayer.

Perhaps most revolutionary of them all, it was someone who led with their weakness, not their strength.

I'm saying there's still a chance!

How I Defied the Odds

When I was in Bible college, I started to have doubts about the faith. It doesn't happen to everyone, but I can recall exactly where I was when it started. I was flying to New Mexico after speaking at a youth event in Arkansas. I used to always sit in the window seat, put on my headphones, look out the window, and pray. Add pretzels and cranberry juice to the mix and it was, for all intents and purposes, Communion with Christ. So I boarded the plane, pressed *play* on my iPod, looked out the window, and felt . . . nothing. For the first time, my thoughts about God were not comforting. If anything, they were working against me.

Why didn't God heal the youth pastor I prayed for yesterday?

Do I even believe the message I spoke?

How stupid am I? Staring out the window, praying to an invisible God.

To say they snowballed is an understatement. Over the next few weeks, I was waking up with more questions. Some historical. Some existential. But all of them unwanted. They trespassed on every positive experience I ever had with God. When I would think about youth camps, I wouldn't remember being called to ministry by the presence of God; I would dwell on the manipulative rhetoric the preacher used. I wasn't called. I was coerced. Going to church became altogether weird. Praise and worship were no longer a time to sing the borrowed prayers of our brothers and sisters. Instead, I observed my friends go into a trance from some Christian version of karaoke. They weren't worshiping. They were brainwashed.

And worst of all was when I was alone. At least in public my doubts were tempered by all the distractions and authentic friendships. When I was alone, I had no hope of recovering. I was leaving the faith one day at a time. It started with not feeling the presence of God, and it progressively turned into not believing there is a presence to be felt. Doubts turned into depression, and depression made me desperate. As you are about to see, I was willing to try just about anything to make my questions go away.

When my pastor found out I was doubting, he called me in his office after service. His office smelled like coffee. The couches were well-kept, and the books aligned on the bookshelf perfectly. It was the type of office that made you address him as Pastor. Even if you would normally be on a first-name basis, not in his office.

"Preston, sit right here." He motioned for some of the available staff to come in.

"Close the door," he said as he laid his hand on my shoulder.

Giving the staff the CliffsNotes version of my struggle was all they needed. They had a second service to get to, after all. The pastor conveyed to them that the enemy of my soul was attacking my belief in God because I was doubting the faith and experiencing bouts of depression. Then they tried to cast out any demon of doubt, followed by telling me to listen to more worship music and sleep on the Bible. You heard that right, they told me to *sleep on the Bible*. Apparently, it was supposed to work like osmosis. "Keep your mind pure," they said. And since I was desperate, I tried all those things.

Maybe it was because I slept on the wrong Bible translation, but as you can imagine, none of it worked. I went from doubting, to depressed, to desperate, to thoroughly disappointed. Disappointed because my suspicions were confirmed. If God wasn't willing to show up when I really needed him, maybe it's because he can't show up. Maybe it's because he is not real.

To be clear, I wasn't just wondering about the existence of God. My understanding of faith and life was breaking down, which eventually deconstructed my entire worldview.

Following my failed deliverance, I went to a doctor. Perhaps something was off with my hormones. Maybe I don't have the capacity to think straight. Maybe I'm sick. I told the doctor about the crazy thoughts I was having and how it was causing me to stay in bed well past noon.

"It's not situational depression," I told him. "There isn't really anything for me to be depressed about."

It felt more permanent than that. I remember even telling the doctor to find something wrong with me. I needed a pill to make my pain go away.

After the blood results came in, the doctor told me that all my levels were fine. This is the report that most people want to hear from the doctor, but not me. All this meant was that I was responsible for handling my doubts and depression. There was no way out other than admitting that they were valid and welcoming them in. I thought the day I invited Jesus into my heart, he would protect me from all the intruders who would come barging in. Apparently, he wasn't in there anymore. Doubt and depression made themselves right at home. At this point, I would have taken either: a pill or a Savior.

The summer was coming to an end, and I knew I couldn't go back to Bible college. But I wanted something to show for my time there. I needed to go back to at least finish my associate's degree. The problem was, I was supposed to be the head resident assistant of a dorm. Imagine that! A doubting spiritual leader praying for you, planning devotionals, and talking theology.

I emailed the resident director to let her know what I was going through. To address the depression, she encouraged me by quoting Scripture and speaking to the potential she saw in my life. As far as the doubting went, not much was said about it, but she did want me to return to the college. I wasn't sure what type of train wreck was ahead, but the conductor gave me the thumbs up, and I needed a degree. I was shy about my unbelief because I knew it wouldn't go over well.

The next part of my journey is a game changer. To quote writer and philosopher Albert Camus: "In the depths of winter, I finally learned that within me there lay an invincible summer."[3] I'm always hesitant to share it for a few reasons. First, some people find divine encounters off-putting, and it ends up discrediting the entire story. If that's you, just remember that I'm naturally very skeptical of supernatural claims, and I totally understand your suspicion. After all, I am the one who started something called "The Doubters' Club." Second, divine encounters are not regular pit stops on our detour away from God. I can't say this will happen to everyone, but it happened to me. All I can say is that authenticity before God was the only option I had left.

I arrived at the dorms in the afternoon and was supposed to be leading a meeting within the hour. Exhausted after bringing in my luggage, I slumped down onto the futon and wept. I was tired of fighting for something I didn't believe in with someone who wasn't there. I didn't know how this was going to look for the next academic year, but none of the outcomes seemed promising. I was a doubter at a Bible college who didn't believe in the Bible. Sick and tired of everything "Christian," here is all I had to say to God:

"God, if you are up there and you don't do something now, I will never come back to you."

It wasn't an ultimatum. That's what you do when you are playing religion and trying to twist God's arm—you give him an ultimatum. This was authentic. This is what one lover says to another when they are tired of the way the other is acting in the relationship. Like a forsaken lover, I cried for what felt like hours. In fact, I cried myself to sleep and missed the meeting entirely.

When I finally woke up, it was three hours later. It's hard to explain how I felt upon waking up that afternoon. Typically, naps help you feel refreshed. This must have been more than a nap because I wasn't just refreshed; I felt renewed. It was a similar sensation to the one you get when you wake up from a nightmare only to realize it was merely a bad dream or the relief that sweeps through your body when you know that your thoughts were not your own and that what is real is better than what you dreamt of. It was like that. Instead of an alarm waking me up, however, it felt like love pouring around me, in me, through me, and for me. I was in love with whatever was visiting my spirit, and it was in love with me.

Looking back, it is similar to when Jesus turned the dirty, foot-washing water into wine at the wedding. The moment he touched the water, it blushed. I was blushing before God in that dorm room. I was embarrassed and invigorated at the same time. Totally embarrassed by my unbelief but invigorated by the acceptance I was experiencing. Even as I write this, it is difficult to say whether that was the day I entered the Kingdom of God again, or the day I crashed into it. C. S. Lewis said he went kicking and screaming into the Kingdom of God, "the most dejected and reluctant convert in all of England."[4] I think I woke up in the Kingdom of God. The most renewed convert in all of Texas.

That experience marked me. I realized that day there is something outside of myself that is wanting to interact with me; and the key to that interaction is not suppressing my doubts, but regarding them as the means to an authentic relationship with whatever it was that woke me up. I did not know at the time that it was Jesus, since the Jesus I was crying out to never answered my prayers. That Jesus died over two thousand years ago, and dead people don't come back to life. Plus, that Jesus rebuked doubters for their unbelief. Or so I thought.

A few days later, a professor of philosophy and apologetics heard about the summer I had had. At the time, I didn't know what apologetics even was. He asked me if he could walk with me through my questions and doubts during some of his office hours.

"Sure." Anything is better than sleeping on the Bible.

Then he said something that indicated he truly cared about me. "I don't care where you land, as long as you're honest. You don't have to end up thinking like me." That conversation began a journey that led to my life's work.

Thinking Differently in the Same Kingdom

To get where we haven't been before, we have to be willing to do what we haven't done before. We have prayed. We have learned apologetics. We have debated, persuaded, and manipulated. What haven't we done? We haven't given the people who doubt Christianity the right to leave *our* version of faith so that they may enter the Kingdom of God.

Perhaps you think the only way in is through the front door as you experienced it.

A service.

A prayer.

A confession.

These methods are making the odds of doubters following Jesus go down, not up. Moreover, did Jesus speak of the Kingdom of God like this? He spoke of it as a reality that exists inside us (Luke 17:21; see ESV note). It is the eternal spiritual reality where God eternally reigns and by which we experience his presence and reign here on earth. If the Kingdom of God is within you, you should leave a little bit of heaven everywhere you go. And I think that is our new strategy. Go to heavenless places and leave a trail of evidence for the doubter. Not through argumentation (sometimes that feels more like hell), but rather by demonstrating that life in Christ is not necessarily thinking like us; it is thinking with us. We are all doubters on a journey to the front door. Doubts, not answers, might be our common ground with the unbeliever.

This understanding led me to start the Doubters' Club. The goal has remained the same since its inception, and it's simple:

Model friendship with people who
think differently and pursue truth together.

Period. There is no praying for one another or liturgical/ structured reading of sacred texts. The whole meeting exists for the people who are not spiritually curious enough to attend church. It is a meeting where Jesus can be brought into conversation without the condemnation they may feel from religion. The goal is not for me to win and them to lose. In fact, to lose a relationship with them is to altogether lose. During the meeting, we talk about whatever topic the group voted on the time before. The topics have ranged from sexuality to the violence of the Old Testament. One time we even talked about whether artificial intelligence will ever have a soul. (I needed a lot of coffee for that meeting.)

Below is the agenda for how we hold a Doubters' Club meeting:

Step 1. We go over our five ground rules so we can have a respectful discussion:

1. We value respect above being right.
2. We listen without interrupting.
3. We are a safe place.
4. We listen with an open mind.
5. We understand and accept differences of opinion.

Step 2. A Christian and an unbeliever talk back and forth about the issue at hand for about ten to fifteen minutes. Since its inception in 2015, we have launched multiple Doubters' Clubs. Some have Christians and universalists. Others have Christians and agnostics. Others have Christians and Jews. To maintain the integrity of the meeting, it doesn't need to have a Christian and an atheist. It just has to be two people who don't think alike.

Remember, we are modeling friendship with people who think differently.

Step 3. After discussion between the two moderators has generated some ideas and brought levity to the room, the topic is opened up for discussion for the next hour. This is when people from all backgrounds and belief systems start sharing their thoughts, asking questions, and building genuine interest in one another. Remember, we are pursuing truth together.

Step 4. Then, we vote on the next month's topic. Attendees offer suggestions for the next discussion topic, then vote by raising their hand when the moderator reads their favorite option. (Imagine an unchurched congregation picking the sermon series.)

The Doubters' Club is a dialogical setting where even people who hate God are welcome to come and air their grievances. Many times, the faith they have walked away from is itself a departure from historic, biblically informed Christianity. It's a faith that is not at all coherent with the world around them. It's not consistent in what it claims. And it doesn't cooperate with someone who thinks differently than them. They have to walk away from that faith if they are going to have any chance of coming into the Kingdom of God. In all honesty, so many of them are part of the Kingdom already. The only difference is that they are still wrestling with God on a few issues that the fundamentalist believer seems to have absolute certainty on. They think differently, but the Kingdom is in them. As they discover truth, the closer they come to truth, the closer they come to God.

In their timely book *The Shaping of Things to Come*, Michael Frost and Alan Hirsch give a helpful illustration here. They make the distinction between fences and wells. Most of evangelical thought about the Kingdom of God is in terms of fences.

"In some farming communities, the farmers might build fences around their properties to keep their livestock in and the livestock of other farms out. This is a bounded set."[5] That is, it keeps track of who's in and who's out. Religions do this in a variety of ways. Church membership rosters are an obvious one. Contrary to a bounded set, a more Christ-centered way of thinking about the Kingdom is by picturing a rural community where farms and ranches cover an enormous geographical location. The area is so vast that fences are out of the question.

> Under these conditions a farmer has to sink a bore and create a well, a precious water supply. . . . It is assumed that livestock, though they will stray, will never roam too far from the well, lest they die. This is a centered set. As long as there remains clean water, the livestock will remain close by.[6]

The diagram below visually illustrates what Hirsch and Frost refer to as the center versus bounded set.

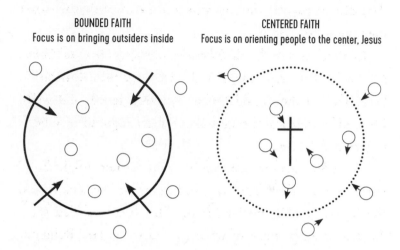

BOUNDED FAITH
Focus is on bringing outsiders inside

CENTERED FAITH
Focus is on orienting people to the center, Jesus

Rather than seeing people as *in* or *out*, what if we started seeing people by their degree of distance from Jesus?

There is a story in the New Testament about a man named Zacchaeus who persisted to see Jesus even though the crowd was boxing him out.

> Then Jesus entered and walked through Jericho. There was a man there, his name Zacchaeus, the head tax man and quite rich. He wanted desperately to see Jesus, but the crowd was in his way—he was a short man and couldn't see over the crowd. So he ran on ahead and climbed up in a sycamore tree so he could see Jesus when he came by.
>
> LUKE 19:1-4, MSG

When Zacchaeus was trying to see Jesus, Scripture tells us that the religious followers were blocking his view. Human fences, if you will. The "wee little man" (sing along if you know it) had to climb a sycamore tree to get a clear view of Jesus. Perhaps our dogmatic approaches to who's in and who's out are obstructing people's view of Jesus. Instead of obstructing people's view, we need to be sycamore-tree planters. We need to be well diggers. We need more spaces like the Doubters' Club. You can be that space.

Being the Kingdom to All

Jesus shows us the way to become a safe space to all the doubters who are walking away from faith in him. In Jesus' day, Jerusalem was the place of faith. The psalmist spoke of it often as a place that got special attention from God. "The LORD builds up Jerusalem; he gathers the exiles of Israel" (Psalm 147:2, NIV). The story is told of two disciples who were returning home after attending Passover in Jerusalem. Journeying away from their faith, these disciples were doubting, depressed, and absolutely disappointed.

Now that same day two of them were going to a village called Emmaus, about seven miles from Jerusalem. They were talking with each other about everything that had happened. As they talked and discussed these things with each other, Jesus himself

came up and walked along with them; but they were
kept from recognizing him.

LUKE 24:13-16, NIV

Walking away from faith, they are now bumping into
the embodiment of the Kingdom of God. Jesus walks along
with them as they continue to move away from the place of
the Resurrection. Commentaries tell us that these two would
have had to be disheartened and full of disbelief about who
Jesus claimed to be.[7] Since Luke frequently reported Jesus
heading toward Jerusalem and his mission on the cross, he
likely intended there to be a stark contrast here. These two
are heading in the opposite direction of Jesus and the fulfill-
ment of his mission. The story continues as Jesus asks them
what they were discussing.

They stood still, their faces downcast. One of them,
named Cleopas, asked him, "Are you the only one
visiting Jerusalem who does not know the things that
have happened there in these days?"

"What things?" he asked.

"About Jesus of Nazareth," they replied. "He was
a prophet, powerful in word and deed before God
and all the people. The chief priests and our rulers
handed him over to be sentenced to death, and
they crucified him; but we had hoped that he was
the one who was going to redeem Israel. And what
is more, it is the third day since all this took place.

In addition, some of our women amazed us. They
went to the tomb early this morning but didn't
find his body. They came and told us that they had
seen a vision of angels, who said he was alive. Then
some of our companions went to the tomb and
found it just as the women had said, but they did
not see Jesus."

LUKE 24:17-24, NIV

Is this not the case for our doubting brothers and sisters?
Or perhaps for ourselves as the doubters in the story. We
are all surrounded by companions who seem to have a more
robust belief than we do, filled with stories of visions and
experiences. Maybe together we would be able to discern the
presence of Christ among us. Maybe that's the point. That no
doubter is left alone to their questions and disappointments.
We are to walk alongside them, slightly confused ourselves.
All the while, looking to recognize the Kingdom of God with
us the whole time.

When he was at the table with them, he took bread,
gave thanks, broke it and began to give it to them.
Then their eyes were opened and they recognized
him, and he disappeared from their sight. They
asked each other, "Were not our hearts burning
within us while he talked with us on the road and
opened the Scriptures to us?"

LUKE 24:30-32, NIV

These not-yet Christians were walking away from the Resurrection only to experience the Kingdom of God in the flesh. But did you notice? It was a slow heart that burned within. With each step, Jesus was by their side and the embers of their hearts grew brighter and brighter. I can just imagine one of them asking the other, "Does your heart burn, too? Jesus was walking with us this whole time! We thought it was over, but it has only just begun."

It is important that we are willing to be the companion who journeys with our doubting friends, recognizing Christ among us and acknowledging his love within us.

Invite Them to the Table

The remainder of the book has practical steps you can take to make the Doubters' Club a lifestyle. To get there, however, you have to be willing to say yes to a question:

Would you be willing to start breaking bread
with the people Jesus broke bread with?

Can you grab coffee with the person you would normally condemn? The people he invited to the table were far from churchgoers. They were religious outcasts. Jesus spent so much time with them he was often thrown in the same category as they were. "The Son of Man has come eating and drinking, and you say, 'Look at him! A glutton and a drunkard, a friend of tax collectors and sinners!'" (Luke 7:34).

It gets worse. Not only will reaching the doubter compromise your reputation, you may never see them decide
to follow Jesus. Remember Judas? He received an invitation
to the table even though Jesus knew how Judas's story was
going to end.

Forget doubter—Judas was a traitor invited to the Lord's
table. The lost cause of the bunch who had ulterior motives
in the relationship. If you say yes to this new way of living
like Jesus, you will be saying yes to being ridiculed by the
religious and rejected by some you invest a lot of time into.
But don't lose heart; this is good news! For I know the depths
Jesus had to go to reach me, and I have lost count of the
times I have betrayed him. To be like Jesus to the doubter, it
is helpful to remember the daily invitation he offers to each
one of us:

Even if you betray me tomorrow,
will you partake of me today?

2

GOD, I'M TIRED OF THIS

The Exhaustion of Only Having Christian Friends

*Walking with a friend in the dark
is better than walking alone in the light.*

HELEN KELLER

Think different.

APPLE

SOME OF MY FRIENDS HAVE told me that we Christians are out of our minds. I prefer to say that we are frenzied and irrational at times, but I get what they are saying. Instead of going back and forth to justify my perspectives and biases, I decided years ago that perhaps one of the best ways to win trust would be through listening to their stories. There is nothing compromising about listening to the experiences people have had with other Christians. And by listening, I mean two ears open, mouth closed, no counterbalancing their story listening. Get through a whole cup of coffee by only asking questions listening. The Proverbs 18:13 type of listening. "If one gives an answer before he hears, it is his folly and shame." What is the impression my friends have of me and my Christian friends? Some people may be surprised and disturbed to find that most of the sentiments unbelievers have of believers are shared by believers as well.

We, too, feel that little can be done to prevent the total collapse of religion into politics. We, too, see a house-of-cards theology sweeping through many churches that are built on anything but life with Christ. We, too, are witnessing how many pastors and churches have been influenced by celebrity culture. Just to name a few. We have to be willing to confess that there is some intrinsic chaos and confusion within the church. My love for the church won't allow me to say that the body of Christ is delirious, but it's not always delightful. Additionally, one of the greatest battlegrounds isn't just in what we have witnessed alongside our unbelieving friends, it's in the shared experiences we have of the church. Our experiences motivate us to ask the same questions.

Why do my non-Christian friends seem more authentic than my Christian friends?

How come there seems to be more grace from unbelievers than believers?

Why are there so many hypocrites in the church?

You have probably heard similar questions from a family member who thinks differently from you. Or perhaps you have asked similar questions yourself. Unfortunately, this has become normal.

Mahatma Gandhi shared the same suspicious spirit. He's often quoted as saying, "I like your Christ, I do not like your Christians. Your Christians are so unlike your Christ." This feeling is shared by just about every unbeliever I know. And if personal interactions are at all indicative of societal trends, those outside the faith are apprehensive of those inside the faith, while those inside the faith are exhausted by the demands of their own in-group. Mostly because the demands of our in-group continue to reinforce a sometimes well-deserved, spoiled reputation derived from perceived and experienced legalisms and dogmas.

Just last Friday I found out my neighbor across the street avoids me because I am employed by a Christian organization. He told another neighbor I was likely to judge him since he "likes to have a beer at the end of the day." I would have laughed out loud if it wasn't true. It's discouraging because there is a real-life story of personal discrimination behind that comment. There is a reason my in-group has that reputation. And what if he asks me about how my organization feels about his habits? Defending that reputation through dogma within doctrines, programs within systems, and systems within institutions, makes me ready to switch jerseys at the end of the day. Only having Christian friends puts you on the defensive when you encounter a doubter, and being on the defensive all the time is exhausting.

You have probably felt the exhaustion of only having Christian friends. You get lumped into the larger stereotype. Guilty by association. All the while, your love for Christ is compelling you to befriend your beer-drinking neighbor. It doesn't feel that simple, though. You know you will have to justify the time spent with "the other" and remind your brothers and sisters that you aren't going to end up an alcoholic. Or gay. Or an atheist. Maybe you are reminded of what your youth pastor said in order to keep the bad ones out of the youth group: Show me your friends, and I'll show you your future. Too much time with them over there and you become like them. So instead, you spent too much time with us over here and became just like your in-group.

Therein lies the problem.

We never wanted to be so defensive about our convictions, but it's the inner victory we think we need to be in the world but not of the world (see John 17:14-19). Us four and no more. It's exhausting, and it is not a victory at all. If we don't overcome the discomfort of befriending people who think, act, and look differently than we do, we will certainly be overcome by a world of people who correctly think they are better off without us.

Stop Being Friendly

Instead of defending the reputation of the flock, what if we returned to the actions of the Shepherd? The Shepherd whose friendship with sinners was so fierce, he was stereotyped as one of them: "The Son of Man came eating and drinking, and they say, 'Here is a glutton and a drunkard, a friend of tax collectors and sinners'" (Matthew 11:19, NIV).

Jesus is a puzzling character study in the area of how we should befriend people. He doesn't play well with the religious people, and he is never too busy to talk to the people everyone else is busy avoiding. Opinion polls don't matter much to him. His political stance is entirely different than any one party. Jesus' selection of friends is based more on those he can help than those who can help him. This may seem obvious to those of us familiar with the Gospels, but remember, we are talking about friends here. We are not merely talking about how he interacted with people. Too often, we think that success in the Christian life is being friendly with sinners. It's a step in the right direction, for sure. Being friendly, however, is not what records show Jesus doing. He was a friend to sinners. As the Word become flesh (John 1:14), Jesus' definition of friends would be the most in line with Scripture. Let's pull back the curtain a bit to see how Jesus lived out true friendship.

Jesus defines a friend as someone who "sticks closer than a brother" (Proverbs 18:24). Brothers can fight it out, but they don't abandon one another based on their differences. Growing up, one of the greatest benefits of having an older brother was that he was the only one allowed to treat me like a younger brother. Meaning, my older brother Shawn made sure that no one else picked on me. He was the barricade between bullies getting to me—a quality we have hardly shown to our wayward, younger brothers (Luke 15). If we befriend the skeptic, one of our massive responsibilities is to defend them and their story in the face of other people's disapproval. Brothers don't always approve of one another, but those are conversations to be had behind closed doors. Being friendly would be acting closer than a brother through nice, even vulnerable, conversations. Being a friend means sticking around when their vulnerability and mistakes tempt you to run the other way.

Jesus defines friendship as laying down your life for another (John 15:13). Laying down your life is anything but a nice gesture; Jesus meant a willingness to die. It's important that we recognize the verb usage. "Laying down" implies intentionality on our part. We are to intentionally be willing to give our lives away for the sake of the other. The likelihood of me needing to literally lay down my life, or die, for my friend may be low from a statistical standpoint. But what is life made of? Life is made up of stuff. Stuff like time, resources, passions, interests, and the like. Accordingly, friends give up these things if it benefits the other party. Being friendly means we are willing to be inconvenienced, for a time, if it helps someone. Being a friend means we readily volunteer what is ours so it can be theirs.

Jesus defines friendship as letting people in on what God is saying. "No longer do I call you servants, for the servant does not know what his master is doing; but I have called you friends, for all that I have heard from my Father I have made known to you" (John 15:15). Friends talk about what they are most passionate about. Since we are passionate about our relationship with Jesus, wouldn't it make sense that at least some of our spiritual energy is devoted to sharing that passion with others? Later in the book, I mention ways we can do this without being weird. Namely, through *invitations* into life and *initiating* conversations that matter. Being friendly doesn't mean we are sharing Jesus in order to close the deal before the conversation ends. Being friends means we are talking about the spiritual aspect of our lives because it is something we are passionate about.

The rest of this chapter could exhaustively explain how Scripture defines friendship. Instead, let's look at how the overarching narrative of friendship in the Bible can be summed up in three categories: association, loyalty, and affection. According to *Baker's Evangelical Dictionary*, these three categories build on themselves to show deeper relationships between the characters we are reading about. It is never shallower than association, though. The biblical words used for friend, companion, or neighbor do not reflect our twenty-first-century understanding of friendship. The primary biblical words used to describe friendships start with the baseline meaning of what it means to be associated with someone. It only builds from there. The richest theological definition we have for friendship is the quality of someone being associated with, loyal to, and having a deep affection for someone else. Notice that the lowest standard for first-century friendship is a high bar for twenty-first-century relationships.[1]

You might recall when Jesus was giving a collection of sayings and teachings to interested listeners in Matthew 5. He intrigued the crowds by first blessing everyone who feels like they are "at the end of [their] rope" (Matthew 5:3, MSG). By everyone, I mean those who did it to themselves *and* those who were just dealt a bad hand. Those "buffeted by the fickle winds of failure, battered by their own unruly emotions, and bruised by rejection and ridicule,"[2] as Brennan Manning describes them. Jesus danced on some first-century land mines by blessing the poor and persecuted. Then, he broadens his blessing to all of us who have been listening to him in the corner with our journal, Bible, and Christian friends. He identifies us as salt. To be honest, the salt-and-light metaphor is one of the most painful passages to apply in all of Scripture. Salt is only useful when in association with things that would, by themselves, lack flavor. It is useless in isolation. And salt is not visibly noticed on food.

Salt must be associated with something that would be flavorless without it.

Salt never takes the credit.

People hardly notice it because there is a blending in quality to it. It's totally associated with whatever it's seasoning. What people notice is the food it is on. When the right amount of salt is used, the food tastes much better! Let me put it this way: Salt doesn't seek attention. It seeks to make whatever it is being sprinkled on so desirable that people come back for more.

Are you willing to be associated with the ones whom your in-group may consider flavorless and undesirable?

Retreating to the Norm

Years ago, some of our friends asked us if we would like to go on a retreat with them to the mountains. They were some of the first Christians to consistently attend the Doubters' Club. I leaned on their wisdom many times when navigating how to answer some of the most emotionally charged questions. Plus, Steve and Whitney had two daughters the same age as ours. Christians who live on mission: check. Friends for our kids to play with: check. A free getaway to a destination location: check. What could possibly go wrong on a retreat to the mountains for two days together?

Steve had a family friend who owned this Airbnb in the mountains of Colorado. It was a house like I have never seen before. In the two days we were there, I don't think I walked into all the rooms. It sleeps twenty-seven people, comfortably. There is a theater room with theater seating and unbelievable surround sound. And if you're not into watching movies, you could just go outside and sit in the hot tub while waving at the skiers as they load the chair lift. This house was at the base of one of the best ski lifts in Colorado! The night we all arrived is when the salty conversation began.

"Preston and Lisa, we are so thankful for all that you are doing through the Doubters' Club, but we had a question about a leader of one of the club locations." Whitney was bouncing her youngest up and down in one arm as she was talking. Having kids around is a good distraction. They allow you to avoid eye contact while trying to have adult conversations.

"Okay," I replied. "What's your question?"

Steve opened his mouth to respond, but before he could speak, Whitney interrupted. I think she thought she could lessen the blow by asking in a more subtle way. "Well . . . Travis is the Christian co-moderator for the second Doubters' Club location, and . . . you know he lives with his fiancée, right? How can someone live with their fiancée and be in leadership? What kind of message does that send?"

It was anything but subtle, but it was a legitimate question. My friends grew up in a conservative, fundamentalist community where certain sins (particularly the public ones) were deal breakers when it came to who could serve in leadership. The difference here, though, is that the Doubters' Club is not a church. It's a club. Travis isn't a leader. He is a co-moderator. Equally co-moderating at his location was an atheist. I explained this distinction to them and told them that there are bits of Travis's story that people don't know.

He came to know Jesus recently, and his fiancée followed shortly after. Travis and his fiancée came from two very different families. He is black, and she is white. Her family isn't just white; they are racist. It's a disturbing, but deserving, label in this case. When they got pregnant out of wedlock, her Christian family encouraged her to have an abortion. It wasn't the unease of having a child outside of marriage that bothered them. You guessed it—it was the embarrassment of having a mixed baby in their family tree. Abort the baby, and abandon the relationship. That was the advice she had received over the phone.

"And if you don't at least break up with him," her dad would tell her, "I'm not sending you any more money. You're on your own."

But she wasn't going to be on her own. She would have a committed man and a beautiful baby boy. Thankfully, she ignored the advice of her bigoted father. Meaning, while they were planning the wedding, they were raising a child. Both of them loved Jesus, loved one another, loved their child, and were pursuing a life together in the process. The question was, how do you plan a wedding when prejudice and intolerance are so strong? Sure, they could have run off and gotten hitched. Or they could see their wedding as an opportunity. A way to declare to both families that God didn't make a mistake when he made them different colors, and the mixing of those two colors in their son wasn't a mistake either. After attending the Doubters' Club together and coming to the church often, they asked me to officiate their wedding. And in the process, Travis wanted to start a Doubters' Club. All this was confidential at the time.

My association with Travis put me under interrogation, while his reputation was questioned because he lived with his fiancée. Which meant my wife and I were going to spend the better half of the entire evening defending ourselves and Travis, without breaking confidentiality about his situation.

"Whitney," I continued. "There is so much more to the story. I know it's cleaner when Christians are living how we prefer, and yes, there are standards for how Christians should live. The Doubters' Club has a standard for the Christian moderator that we don't talk about in Christian-leadership circles. Namely, having genuine relationships with non-Christians. You'll have to trust that there is much more going on than just someone having sex out of wedlock."

The most poignant moment came when Steve tried to give a simplistic diagnosis to a very complex situation. "We just want to make sure you have standards for Christian leaders, Preston. What are your requirements that make someone fit to be a leader?" There it was. I was now being lumped with the leaders who have no standards. Twenty-seven beds in that place, and not one of them would make me feel comfortable enough to sleep there.

Few things are better at providing answers that can soothe an already shattered faith than a perceptive wife. Lisa has taught me to grow in patience toward my own in-group. It's a superpower, really. The calm to my angry Hulk moments. She has oftentimes reminded me of something I want to remind you of: You do not need to spend needless energy justifying your association with people who are not like you. Instead, expend your energy on those people by being *with* and *for* them. The best way to justify your time with those not like your in-group might just be to get crucified by your own in-group. Sometimes, the out-group you were holding ground for will take up your cross and follow your way of living.

Make It Personal

At the time of writing this book, the world is in the middle of the coronavirus pandemic while riots and protests over George Floyd's death are filling the streets. Writing a book about befriending those who are not like you has never felt more appropriate, but it has been very challenging. It's hard to keep your hands to the plow when you aren't sure if the next season will grow the crops or if the field will be burned (Luke 9:62). In all reality, the Doubters' Club alone won't heal the world, but it can be our part in the healing.

Be it racism, religion, or radical ideologies, we are always faced with one of three options when interacting with people not like us: politicize them, generalize them, or personalize the relationship at hand.

We must not politicize it. The quickest way to suck God's justice out of a room is by politicizing it. An issue can be so encrusted with so many layers of politicization that we can hardly see a human being on the other side. Politics have certainly charged topics such as poverty and sexuality. What we often forget in the discussion is that issues are always raised by a person or about a person. If we keep people at the heart of the discussion, we will rarely see their unique situation through the eyes of our political party (if we even have one). Paul wrote, "There is neither Jew nor Greek, there is neither slave nor free, there is no male and female" (Galatians 3:28); I think we can rightly echo those words by saying, "There is also neither blue nor red." *People are not bipartisan issues.*

And this has always been God's heart, long before he revealed himself in Christ.

> When Joshua was by Jericho, he lifted up his eyes and looked, and behold, a man was standing before him with his drawn sword in his hand. And Joshua went to him and said to him, "Are you for us, or for our adversaries?" And he said, "No; but I am the commander of the army of the LORD. Now I have come." And Joshua fell on his face to the earth and worshiped and said to him, "What does my lord say to his servant?" And the commander of the LORD's army said to Joshua, "Take off your sandals from your feet, for the place where you are standing is holy." And Joshua did so.
>
> JOSHUA 5:13-15

What a question! "Lord, are you for us, or for our adversaries?" "No."

The question is not what side is God on. The question is whether we are on God's side. He is a side all by himself. Holy. Distinctly other. Those who are with him are constantly on holy ground. Heaven's embassy welcomes all who would choose to be a part of God's side. Just take off your shoes on the way in. Let's keep the dirty politics out of it. People are here. Not politics.

We must not generalize it. No one likes to be lumped with oversimplifications about the issues at hand in order to fit a preferred narrative. People can have thoughts that don't fit. In fact, if we are going to have any chance at people changing their minds as we pursue truth with them, it will require some level of cognitive dissonance, knowing that some level of inconsistent beliefs or thoughts exist that don't line up with practice. In the past, this has been the "gotcha" moment for most Christians. We would point out the inconsistency only to back the atheist into a philosophical corner, showing where the person's stance on a particular idea doesn't line up with the general confession of their worldview. Should it surprise us that generalizations don't win others over? Do any of us want to fit the stereotype of our in-group?

When launching the Springfield Doubters' Club location, a member of the Freethinkers in Springfield (an organization for individuals who don't subscribe to a particular religion or way of thinking) publicly posted about me. She assumed I was "just like the other Christians in the Bible Belt," stating that there is never a time Christians can host gatherings with non-Christians without trying to convert the non-Christians. Generally, she is correct. But the Doubters' Club doesn't fit into that generalization. After attending the Doubters' Club meeting, one of the leaders of the Freethinkers group told me that he "found it to be a really good thing." He continued to attend, and even helped host some of the meetings.

It's often the case that when you get people talking about issues that matter, many times their thoughts don't align with their cause. To the strict materialist, love and justice are of the utmost importance, even though those are immaterial concepts. Human dignity is more important than animal rights to an atheist, even though humans should have no more intrinsic worth than animals, according to this worldview. It's important not to make assumptions about what a person who doesn't think like you values.

We must personalize the relationship at hand. It's why I hope the handshake outlives the coronavirus. Dr. Fauci, one of the most prominent voices during the coronavirus pandemic, says the days of handshaking are numbered. "As a society, just forget about shaking hands," he said. "We don't need to shake hands. We've got to break that custom."[3]

Some customs need to be preserved, Dr. Fauci.

There is something profoundly symbolic about two hands joining as the first interaction we have with someone we don't know. We acknowledge unity before we engage with our differences. Personalizing the relationship really means we are willing to listen to their story, carry their burdens, and help them find freedom from the pressure they feel in life.

You Are a *Toy*!

Just in case you were wondering how all your toys went missing as a kid, according to the 1995 computer-animated film *Toy Story*, they came alive! The movie will always live on in Hollywood as a buddy comedy film, but it had a much more profound story to it. The two main characters, Woody and Buzz, will always be iconic figures for the millennial generation. By always, I mean "to infinity and beyond!"

Do you remember the first half of the movie? Woody thinks he has a pretty good life as Andy's favorite toy. Woody also shows who his preferred choice is by constantly reminding Andy, "You're my favorite deputy." The beloved cowboy sheriff faces a challenge, however, when Andy's birthday party reveals that an outsider might have special treatment. The new toy, Buzz Lightyear, space ranger, is here to stay. Woody thought he was the favorite. The chosen one. The answer to indoor, rainy days with nothing else to do. The attention starts to shift to Buzz as he shows the other toys that the sky is the limit. He doesn't believe he is a toy. He believes what he wants to believe, and everyone finds that slightly more compelling than the routine laws of the land enforced by the sheriff.

Woody is overwhelmed with jealousy and tries to get rid of Buzz. In doing so, they both get lost. Perhaps this is where the story comes to life for most Christians. From ancient Near Eastern times with Israel to the Jewish Pharisees of the New Testament and beyond, we have fancied our in-group and been threatened by the outsider. To get rid of the outsider, we have responded like Woody did. We yell at them. We tell them their subjective views of life aren't real. They can't just believe whatever they want and live that way. "Buzz," Woody says, "You are a child's plaything!" He is right. And we might be right too. But by yelling at those who think differently than us, we end up losing ourselves—and our could-have-been friends.

Convinced of our rightness and their wrongness, we throw

pity parties at the proverbial Pizza Planet about how they've ruined our schools and our neighborhoods. Meanwhile, they are looking at us with a sort of tempered anger. Somewhat sympathetically, they see us as stuck in the small-mindedness of the toy box. Buzz puts it perfectly: "You are a sad, strange little man and you have my pity. Farewell."

When we try to get rid of the outsider by screaming about how wrong they are, we alienate them from ourselves. The truth of the movie is that Woody and Buzz need one another. Buzz ends up believing Woody and accepting what he was made to do. Yet, I believe that the movie is more about Woody's change of heart than Buzz's. Woody has a seismic shift in how he thinks about his relationship with Andy and Andy's other toys. The first *Toy Story* movie sums up twenty-first-century Western Christianity in a post-modern culture to a tee. We have been stuck at a standstill with our differences, and Andy wants us both to come home. He will be sad if it's one without the other.

This has always been the heart of the Doubters' Club. As friends, we can pursue truth together. In the next part of this book, I'll explain the most practical approach to befriending someone who thinks differently than you. I guarantee that by the end of chapter 8, you'll be singing, "You've got a friend in me" with the person who doesn't think like you.

3

GOD OF THE DETOUR

You Cannot Clean Up What Was Meant to Be Messy

We should not judge people by their peak of excellence;
but by the distance they have traveled from
the point where they started.

HENRY WARD BEECHER

Roads? Where we're going, we don't need roads!

DOC, *Back to the Future*

THERE ARE OVER SEVENTY DISTINCTLY unique neighborhoods within Denver proper, and I had less than two days to figure out which one of those neighborhoods we were going to move to in order to start a church. My wife, Lisa, and I were living in the Dallas area at the time. We had a daughter who was two and another baby girl on the way. Since Lisa was eight months' pregnant, she couldn't make the trip with me to Denver to find our new community. (Apparently, the car is not the best place to have a baby.) She had confidence in me to find the right neighborhood for our family, and she sent me off with a smile. That's the first time in our marriage that her smile seemed heavy. There is a weight to doing things without your best friend. Nevertheless, I loaded our old Corolla with three trusted friends, an energetic enthusiasm for the unknown, and a playlist that makes a twelve-hour road trip somewhat bearable. Except for the periodic Country song required from one of the other passengers.

My dad met us in Evergreen, Colorado, to welcome us into a family cabin he owned in the mountains, just forty-five minutes outside of the Denver city limits. We were exhausted the next day, but we had to explore. Our journey started with burgers in one of the four major neighborhoods in northwest Denver. Lamb burgers with goat cheese, to be exact. The fries were late to the table, but the taste made up for their delayed timing. I usually don't mind waiting for food, unless I'm in a hurry. We had to start heading back to Dallas in less than twenty-four hours. The next time I was going to be in Denver would be with a U-Haul, two kids, and my (hopefully) still-smiling wife.

"Preston, why don't we see if there is a place to get some coffee before we head to another neighborhood?" My dad gets coffee at the most peculiar times. I can always count on his Starbucks runs in the middle of the afternoon to be the break I need from crowded family gatherings and boring Judge Judy reruns. This time, however, we were in the city. We weren't going to get in the car, only to spend more time trying to find another place to park. Plus, urban dwellers don't go to Starbucks. They support the local coffee shop, who supports the local farmer by using local milk. All of which makes the price of your typical latte go way up. Be that as it may, when in Rome . . . you walk.

That's the coffee shop where I met my atheist friend. The others were looking at a map of the city to make our trip more efficient when I asked the coffee-shop owner what type of church he goes to.

My church-going friends were looking for the most efficient route to tour the city, but it was the detour into the local coffee shop that mattered most. I was there to find a neighborhood. Instead, I found a neighbor. A neighbor who became a friend.

Detours make the journey deeply personal. Detours disorient and reorient, at the same time. They can be caused by suffering a loss of some sort, discovering a new joy, or walking into the local coffee shop.

We are formed more by the detours in life than by the predetermined paths others try to set for us. Take my atheist, coffee-shop-owner friend as an example. When his sister got cancer and his Catholic prayers were to no avail, the path of religion started to feel more like a desert than a wellspring of life. Consequently, he is on the roundabout. Things are taking a little longer. It's not the most efficient route to Christ. Which makes me simultaneously ask two terrible questions: *Have we made an idol out of efficiency?* And, *Is anyone on the predetermined path?*

Yes and no.

We are all shaped by the experiences and events that we

didn't see coming. The detours. The scenic routes. If that is true, what an awful thing to be on a long trip by yourself, altogether disoriented by life! Life is hard, and it should not be done without friendships. Whether someone converts to your way of thinking shouldn't determine whether you remain friends. We all deserve better than a religious rent-a-friend who treats people as means to an end.

Detour Guides

Let's face it, the most beautiful and awful endeavors have been done in the name of God. Not a Doubters' Club meeting goes by that I'm not reminded of the Crusades and the larger-than-life lifestyles of those who unscrupulously collected money from the oppressed. Many of us have found comfort in our faith. Others have found despair. To some, it's a shelter. To others, it's a storm. The sobering reality of religious intentions was summed up well by the fourteenth-century Persian poet Hafiz when he wrote, "The Great religions are the Ships, / Poets the life Boats. / Every sane person I know has jumped / Overboard."[1]

People we love will oftentimes choose to jump overboard, and our response in that moment has the potential to win influence or reinforce any spiritual trauma that knocked them off course in the first place. When I was disrupted by doubts and questions, I needed a thoughtful mind and a hopeful heart. The professor I mentioned earlier listened to my disbelief in the Bible and all things Christian. And when he did speak, it was as someone who knew the power of companionship and the necessity of friendship without ulterior motives. His assurance, "I don't care where you land as long as you're honest," is the language of someone who is committed to the detour, regardless of the destination. Of course, he wanted me to believe in God and follow Jesus. His friendship, however, wasn't based on whether that happened. He was truly my detour guide.

The Jesus of the Gospels is compelling for this very reason. He was a detour guide in a tour-guide profession. Tour guides inform guests about items of historical and cultural importance on an organized, predetermined route. Jesus' peers were convinced they knew the most efficient route to pleasing God and saving people. Detour guides, on the other hand, give companionship to the spiritually homeless. This intentional companionship may influence them toward a predetermined destination—or it may not. One is conditional, the other is committed despite the conditions.

Have we become tour guides to the world?

We go from soapbox to soapbox, pontificating the rightness of our historical faith, treating the world like visitors in a museum. We ooh and aah through the organizational structure of a building, leadership pipelines, and other highly efficient models that build cultural cooperation. I don't know about you, but museum tours aren't nearly as exciting as self-guided tours. And what fun are self-guided tours without an ally who shares in the excitement!

Inquisitive people prefer the "enter at your own risk" type

of adventures. Their curiosity attracts them to the "Do not trespass" signs. "Don't try this at home" is a legal safety net; it actually means "Be careful." Would you consider yourself part of this crowd? If so, we are not rebellious, just human. J. R. R. Tolkien knew something of the human spirit; he wrote, "Not all those who wander are lost."[2] Wandering is unavoidable.

Not desirable; just unavoidable.

Not justified; just unavoidable.

Not the Christian, or non-Christian, thing to do; just unavoidable.

We are, as Robert Robinson wrote in 1758, "prone to wander."

Lord, I feel it.[3]

I'll speak on behalf of the Christians I know, myself included. Most of us are restless, on-the-go vagabonds who are unsettled in most things outside of life with Jesus. Personally, I've moved so many times you could respectfully call me a gypsy. My parenting techniques are less consistent than my breakfast routine. My friends are transient. My love is errant. And I lost my wedding ring . . . again.

Real life is not a tour. Tours are nice and organized. Comfortable and planned. They are administered by someone who knows all the answers to the questions. The longer we pretend to be tour guides, the more evident it will become that we are pretending. All our routes are messy. We are marked by the same sufferings, pains, and questions as everyone else. We wonder where our money goes. We worry about visits to the doctor. And we raise our voice when trying to put the kids to bed. Don't misunderstand me: Following Jesus certainly makes a difference in our lives. His life, death, and resurrection have restored us to God and to the world. All the same, our paths are anything but clean and perfectly planned.

Follow the interactions between Jesus and the crowds and you will quickly find that the adage is true: "The church is a hospital for sinners, not a museum for the saints." At best, we are wounded healers. Wounded by the detours; healed by the Guide. Since this is the case, we must be willing to spend enough time with unbelievers to ruin any reputation we may have with the tour guides of our day. By doing so, we will become more like Jesus.

On a Scale of One to Ten

In 1975, a man named James F. Engel published a book entitled *What's Gone Wrong with the Harvest?* that explored evangelical evangelism methods of the time.[4] Basing much of his idea on behavioral science, Engel suggests a new way to look at a person's spiritual journey toward life in Christ: the Engel Scale. Insight drawn from the Engel Scale sheds light on how someone else views evangelism and discipleship. Instead of the two being different categories or stages in someone's journey toward Christ, the Engel Scale presents growth as a continuum.[5] What if evangelism is not separate from discipleship but part of it?

The scale represents someone's journey from zero to ten; zero being salvation and ten being someone who chooses to live sacrificially, surrendered to the mission of God. Most churches treat discipleship as the process of someone going from a zero to a ten. From next-step classes to mission trips, the goal is to become more like Jesus. As Doubters' Clubs multiplied, I simplified the scale for training purposes. See the simplified scale below for clarity:

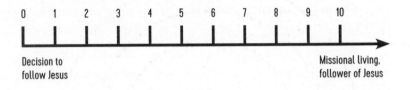

0 1 2 3 4 5 6 7 8 9 10

Decision to
follow Jesus

Missional living,
follower of Jesus

As far as number lines are concerned, for every positive number, there is a negative one. There are negative tens who avoid any hint of spirituality. Mainly, any spirituality that would believe in a Jesus-looking God. This means that the continuum doesn't start at zero. Discipleship starts pre-conversion. Evangelism (or the moment of conversion) happens within discipleship, but it's a long trek from negative ten to zero. A voyage filled with unexpected life events. Mishaps and missteps. Church attendance isn't part of the equation until around negative five, when people are spiritually curious. Hopefully we will see people reach zero, but it's not always the case.

Thus far in the book, we have tethered the Doubters'

Club model of living to Hirsch and Frost's center versus bounded set as well as the Engel Scale. Both cognitive models help us understand that (1) discipleship is about getting people closer to the center (Jesus), and (2) progress to the center happens through relationship. I have combined the two models into a "Doubt to Discipleship" diagram:

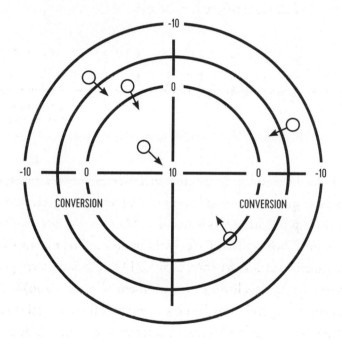

I'm encouraged that the apostle Paul saw people's detours toward God in a similar way. When speaking to the believers in Corinth, he reminded them that he didn't take their salvation on his shoulders. That was not his responsibility.

Instead, he recognized the importance of merely being a Christian who befriended them before they believed.

> I planted the seed, Apollos watered the plants, but *God* made you grow. It's not the one who plants or the one who waters who is at the center of this process but God, who makes things grow. Planting and watering are menial servant jobs at minimum wages. What makes them worth doing is the God we are serving. You happen to be God's field in which we are working.
>
> I CORINTHIANS 3:6-9, MSG

You should meet my old friend Roger from Denver. He had a long beard down to the middle of his chest. It was colored perfectly grey and black—the perfect mix between "I've experienced some life" and "I still have some youth in me." Roger used to be part of a biker gang. Still rockin' that biker look, he now spent most of his time evangelizing in bars and at biker stops. He was a zealous believer. Maybe *feisty* would be a better adjective than *zealous*. He was eager to share Jesus with people and still a little rough around the edges. When I read about Peter in the New Testament, I think about how he and Roger will hit it off someday.

Roger pulled me aside after we had a meeting with all those who were part of the launch team for the church plant we were starting. He let me know that he was choosing to leave the team due to my theology about discipleship. I invited him to talk it through, knowing that whatever it was, we could either agree or at least support one another in our differences.

"You said discipleship starts preconversion, right?" Roger was referring to the Engel Scale illustration mentioned above.

"That's right," I responded. "Is that what you have a problem with?"

"Yes!" He was very evangelistic and didn't like the idea of evangelism not having its own seat at the table.

"Well, Roger. When did the disciples get saved?" I asked. "That is, when did they have the Spirit of Christ living in them?"

"It would have had to have been after Jesus rose from the dead," he replied.

My question had a second part to it. "So, what was Jesus doing for the three years he was on earth with them?"

We both knew the answer, but he still thought for a minute.

"That's not fair!" Roger stated. Followed quickly by "I guess he was discipling them."

Understanding that discipleship starts in whatever context the person's in is critical to being effective with doubters and "detourers." Not just them, but as detour guides, we will quickly find that it's God's growth plan for us as well.

The Meat Is in the Street

It would make sense that the closer a believer gets to a ten on the Engel Scale, the more they would find themselves interacting with those on the negative side of the scale. If an "E10" means living fully as Christ lived, it's safe to assume that the closer we move toward a ten, the more sacrificial we become. Then the question arises: *Who are we sacrificing for as we become more like Christ?* Taking our cues from Jesus, we are sacrificing for the person/people who don't yet consciously participate in the Kingdom of God, the ones who don't think like us. Meaning, in order to fully orient our lives around Jesus, we must be willing to orient our lives around those who don't know him. Even the most theologically apathetic believer would have to acknowledge that the closer we get to the heart of God, the closer we often find ourselves getting to the prodigal. This is where it benefits us to broaden our view of discipleship. Discipleship looks different on the positive side of the scale than it does on the negative side. On the positive side of the Engel Scale, it's to move closer to God's heart and to allow him to soften our heart toward those who are far from him. On the negative side, it's to address negative impressions of Jesus, guide the nonbeliever toward an intention related to Jesus, and create spiritual pathways that allow the nonbeliever to take next steps within the context of trusting relationships. Discipleship on the negative side of the Engel Scale is the focus of this book. Specifically, how the believer can create pathways for the nonbeliever so they can both journey toward Christ together. The believer toward a ten, and the nonbeliever toward a zero (remember, zero is the point of conversion). Throughout the book, I will refer to this pathway as "the Five *Is*." The Five *Is* are:

Impression—how to rebuild the impression another
person has of you;

Intention—how to renovate the intentions you have of
a nonbeliever;

Invitation—how to invite a nonbeliever into real life,
not a church service;

Initiation—how to re-examine our views through
conversations that matter; and

Imitation—how to redefine progress.

A famous Vineyard pastor, John Wimber, contributed to
the larger body of Christ by teaching others how to manifest
the power of the Holy Spirit. Although I am not a Vineyard
minister, and although I never had the honor of meeting
Wimber, it was one small phrase of his that fire-branded my
soul. In reference to sharing Christ with those who do not
know him, Wimber coined the phrase "The meat is in the
street." Good luck trying to forget that pithy, cleverly structured six-word phrase. In my estimation, it is truly the best
way to summarize what the author of Hebrews was saying at
the end of chapter 5.

Though by this time you ought to be teachers, you
need someone to teach you again the basic principles
of the oracles of God. You need milk, not solid food,
for everyone who lives on milk is unskilled in the
word of righteousness, since he is a child. But solid
food is for the mature, for those who have their

powers of discernment trained by constant practice
to distinguish good from evil.

HEBREWS 5:12-14

It's one of the most jarring statements for those who
are addicted to the high of being right: Deeper doctrine is
spiritual milk. Scripture memorization is, at best, 1% milk.
Apologetics is like whole milk, but is milk, nonetheless. The
author of Hebrews clearly sees everyone who is still on milk
as those who are not experienced in what they are learning. Milk is the deepest, most profound truths of Scripture
unapplied.

All the amens without the alleyways.

Scripture without sacrifice.

Doctrine without accompanying the person on the
detour.

We are still on milk if reading this book gets us more
jazzed than living it out.

The meat is truly in the street. Solid food is for the full-
grown believer who, through *constant practice*, is learning.
It is spiritually mature to constantly practice and learn.
Constant seems to entail that it's not a single event. It's not
a short-lived conversation. *Constant* is an adjective that we
Christians aren't well-known for. The ongoing, insistent,
unending quality about what we are doing.

Practice is the doing. It's a curious word selection, as it
paints the picture of a person who has yet to perfect the
thing they are practicing. Never a home run, but still getting

up to bat. Of all the things to practice, love is the most well-rehearsed play for Christ and his followers. The mature in Christ make unending attempts at love.

And then there is the learning piece. It's a posture of humility. As if the experience has something to teach us. The best part of *Kung Fu Panda* is when Oogway, a tortoise karate master, tells Shifu, "One often meets his destiny on the road he takes to avoid it." Practicing love with the atheist and agnostic will help us find Christ.

"What you have done for the least of these," Jesus said, "you have done for me" (Matthew 25:40, author's paraphrase). If you think the skeptic is among the least of those, practice unending love.

Three Pastors and a Lesbian

It's not a setup for a bad joke. This story really happened.

My friends and I were taking an Uber to a local pizza place after attending a missions conference in Houston, Texas. All three of us were church planters, which means we split the fourteen-dollar charge for the Uber. It was supposed to be a quick ride to the destination; however, interruptions are like detours. They slow us down, making us "ruthlessly eliminate hurry," as Dallas Willard puts it.[6]

Playing in the background over the hum of the engine was a sermon by Joel Osteen. The three of us used this as an opportunity to talk with the driver about her faith. We acted like we weren't familiar with the world-renowned preacher.

"You've never heard of Joel Osteen?" It was almost unnerving to our Uber driver that we didn't know who Joel was.

To avoid lying, I asked her what her thoughts about God were.

"You must be a religious person if you're listening to preaching while driving," I said.

"I'm anything but religious," she responded. "I've had a major problem with God most of my life. When I was younger, my dad would teach us about God, take us to church, and even serve as a leader. As I grew up, I noticed how my dad's actions weren't normal." Her voice grew shaky. She was thinking about whether to trust three complete strangers with her story. Fourteen dollars now seemed cheap for the priceless interaction we were about to have.

"My dad raped me growing up," she continued. "He would use his belief in God to justify his forgiveness in between the times he sexually assaulted me. I couldn't question my dad because he was a 'man of God.' So, no . . . I am not religious. The idea of God coming as a man to the world is vile. I don't trust men at all. Especially godly men." At this point we pulled into the pizza parlor's parking lot. The silence in the car was spine-chilling. She turned the Uber app off, but she wasn't done disputing my assumption that she was religious.

"It's probably no surprise that I'm a lesbian now. After all, I never thought I would take part in anything religious. But Joel Osteen isn't religious. He talks about God as Jesus, and

Jesus seems to be the only man I can get close to. He protects me. He doesn't hurt me."

In his book *God in Search of Man*, Polish-born American rabbi Abraham Heschel rightly stated, "When religion speaks only in the name of authority rather than with the voice of compassion—its message becomes meaningless."[7] Never has the message of a Jesus-looking God become more meaningful than in that car. We were all in tears, overcome with compassion for the tender heart in the driver's seat.

Sharing a similar shakiness in his voice, my friend spoke up. "Thank you for sharing that with us. All three of us are pastors. We plant churches for people like you who have a hard time with God."

"You are pastors, and you have never heard of Joel Osteen?"

The tears, joy, laughter. It all felt holy.

"We have heard of him," my friend Zac continued. "We just wanted to hear your story. Before we get out of the car, will you do us all a favor? Will you pray for us?"

She tried turning down his request based on the fact that we were the pastors. If anything, she expected us to pray for her. I've learned over time that ministerial credentials don't matter in Uber cars. In that moment, she was more qualified to pray than any seminary graduate. Zac was right to call her prayer a favor. Favor makes up the bulk of the word *favorite*, and our Uber driver was Jesus' favorite type of person: someone who accepts being found by God, in Christ. We all held hands, and our newfound lesbian friend prayed over us certainty-seeking pastors. Her prayer reminds me of the sign hanging in my kids' upstairs playroom: Broken crayons still color.

In moments like this, the temptation is to speak clear theology and end the car ride with prayer. That's what the tour guides do. They connect the dots for people. Possibly even entering the pizza parlor with a testimony of evangelism to share with other pastors. Not so with detour guides. Detour guides don't connect the dots before they collect the dots. "What is the story?" they ask. God says everything will work together for the good (Romans 8:28), and detour guides aren't shocked to find out what the everything is before connecting it to the good. How we understand the story will always determine our role in it.

By listening through ears of compassion, we practice love. And by practicing love, we are going from milk to meat. When we lean into sacred moments of grace and tenderness together with the other, we are experiencing Christ and becoming more like him in the process.

4

IMPRESSION

How to Rebuild Someone's Impression of You

Sometimes the nicest people you meet are covered in tattoos,
and sometimes the most judgmental people you meet
go to church on Sundays.

EARL DIBBLES JR.

Shade never made anybody less gay.

TAYLOR SWIFT

HAVE YOU EVER MADE SUCH A massive mistake early on that it affected the trajectory of your life?

Mine was when I was fifteen years old. My best friend, Cameron, and I were playing video games. *Dynasty Warriors* on PlayStation 2, to be exact. His house was a second home for me. My house was more like a first home for him. Playing video games together was supposed to be one of the safest places in the world for us. A freezer full of Otter Pops, pizza rolls, the occasional fruit or vegetable, and a metabolism that didn't know the difference. Like many fifteen-year-old boys, most of our conversations revolved around girls. Today's episode: how to trick a girl who would otherwise never want to into kissing you.

"Do you think next time we are all together, we could play truth or dare, and you could dare me to kiss Heather?" I asked. I had braces, frosted tips, and made my own hemp necklaces. How else was I ever going to kiss a girl outside of truth or dare?

"Sure," Cameron laughed. He was clearly more interested in the punch/kick combo than our conversation. I thought it was because he and his girlfriend, Stacey, had been dating for over a year. Of course they had already kissed by now.

"Have you kissed Stacey yet? I bet . . ."

He pushed pause. "No. And I don't want you to dare me to, either."

"Why? She's pretty." My prepubescent mind had two categories: pretty and not pretty. I will never let my daughters date the fifteen-year-old version of me.

"Preston, you promise not to tell anyone? I haven't told any of our other friends."

I unpaused the video game. "Of course."

"The truth is, I don't find her all that attractive. And I have had another relationship outside of Stacey for the past six months. I met him in an online chatroom. He lives here in Albuquerque. Stacey doesn't know, and she can't know. No one can!" Cameron went on to tell me that he found her personality attractive, but he had never found her physically attractive. He wasn't physically attracted to any girl, for that matter.

Unfortunately, Cameron and I both remember what happened next. I pushed the pause button, stood up, and walked out of his house. It was terrible. I can't imagine the thoughts he must have been thinking for the two hours between when I left and when his dad was supposed to get home from work. The uneaten food, unplayed levels, and unfinished confession made it one of the most unsafe places for him. I didn't just leave him with a messy house; I left him a total wreck.

If I had a do-over in life, I would go back to this moment.

I would pause the game only to give him my full attention. To show that our friendship wouldn't skip a beat just because he liked boys and I liked girls. I would make another round of pizza rolls to talk about the difficulties surrounding his situation. I would do anything other than what I did, so his impression of Christian friends wouldn't become what it is today. Today, Cameron is an atheist living in New York City. He didn't just lose one friend that day; when I walked out on him during that vulnerable moment, I took half our friends with me in the name of Christian purity.

At some point, we all must acknowledge the candor of American novelist Cynthia Ozick's words: "Two things remain irretrievable: time and a first impression."[1]

One of my life coaches attributes that day as the reason I am so passionate about the mission of the Doubters' Club. I have a personal vendetta against the repulsive impressions people have of Jesus because of Christians like my fifteen-year-old self. As you know by now, the Doubters' Club is a group of people who refuse to walk out on one another. And if we are going to make this a lifestyle, we have to start with the first *I* of preconversion discipleship. We must all have a personal vendetta against our un-Christlike first *impressions*.

Poisonous Beauty

In the exhaustion of early parenthood, I quickly realized that I had become my child's best friend. That means that I am responsible for keeping them alive and keeping them entertained, at the same time. Making them eat their vegetables and planning an ice-cream outing afterward. Putting them to bed bathed and waking up ready to wrestle. Lathering on the dreaded sunscreen and playing unashamedly in the pool. Children are a huge gift to all of us. They teach some people to take life more seriously because they have to supervise the helpless littles in the room. Others, they teach to not take life so seriously because a significant amount of play needs to take place before 8:00 p.m. One of my favorite times to be a parent is when my kids and I can both share in an experience of learning. American entrepreneur and motivational speaker Jim Rohn spoke of this when he said, "Learn to get excited like a child. There is nothing that has more magic than childish excitement."[2] It's pure magic! There is nothing like when a thirty-three-year-old dad can learn something with his five-year-old daughter. That's why we go to the Wonders of Wildlife National Museum & Aquarium in Springfield, Missouri.

One of the most interesting exhibits there is the poison dart frog. Did you know that some types of this frog have enough venom to kill ten grown men?[3] By merely touching the toxin-filled sweat beads on its body, humans can topple over. Although it is brilliant to look at, it is one of the most dangerous animals on the planet. My daughters and I like to stare at them from the other side of the glass. We name them according to their coloring: Yellow Belly. Golden Eye. Blue's Clues. It's the exhibit where we find ourselves always learning together. "The tree frogs!" We race to find the first one. Our first time visiting the museum, one of the volunteers told us that these particular poison dart frogs used to be poisonous but are not dangerous at all now. "So we can keep one if we want to?" my five-year-old asked.

The peculiar thing about poison dart frogs is that their toxicity comes from their diet.[4] So if they aren't eating prey that assimilates plant poison, they are safe. Swap out the beetles and termites from the Amazon with your local PetSmart cricket paste, wait long enough, and you have a toxic-free frog. What an incredible species! The impression we get from these paperclip-sized killers is that we can come close to them, hold them, or play with them. It's a misleading impression. What they have engorged themselves with will determine whether they are playful or deadly on any given day.

As a director with the Church Multiplication Network, I see a lot of church websites and marketing campaigns. To some degree, it is necessary. What good is a local church if people are not aware that it exists? I can say with certainty that every church planter puts forward a very attractive image about their faith community. The graphics are stunning. The colors are beautiful. The words are inviting. The message is hopeful. I would venture to say that as people look from the other side of the glass, the church looks attractive. It's when the nonchurchgoer gets too close, and perhaps even starts serving, that things start to unravel. We encountered these people in the Doubters' Club all the time. They attended a church based on what was promised from a distance, but they got severely poisoned when they went from spectator to participant. In some cases, it killed their faith. Others are on spiritual life support. The diagnosis? The Christians they were interacting with had a spiritual diet that was poisonous to the outsider. The impression was off.

You Are What You Eat

Matthew is an atheist co-moderator for one of the Doubters' Club locations. I asked him about his thoughts on the Christian faith, and he told me that the impression he gets from Christians doesn't line up with his experiences with them. "There are too many nuances to their beliefs," he said. He's attracted to Christianity from a distance. When he gets too close, he is disoriented with how he feels after having conversations with actual Christians. The common consensus from Matthew and others is that since we are so full of knowledge, it leaves no room for listening and growth. The knowledge we have been consuming feels more or less like poison to the outsider.

We are full of it . . . literally.

The things we talk about have become a predictable poison: how to apply spiritual pressure, how to stand for what we are against instead of being known by what we are for, what political party aligns most with the Kingdom, and why we have all the answers. I put the above statements in a DIET acronym to help us remember the diet that is ruining our impressions:

- Do you know where you are going?
- I disagree with you.
- Enter the voting booth.
- Thanks for asking.

Do you know where you are going?

It's the age-old question that makes so many of us feel like we have to apply enough spiritual pressure to close the deal. What would happen if this unsaved person got in a car crash on the way home? How can they believe in the gospel unless they hear it? Isn't it unloving to not tell people about their sin?

Pressure works in one of two ways: It either pushes in or pulls out. The spiritual pressure we are used to exerting tries to push people into belief. Or push people over at the altar. Or push someone to make a decision based on their vulnerable state. If we aren't careful, we might be pushing people into captivity when the whole Jesus story is about pulling them out. I don't think it is wrong to apply spiritual pressure. I just think it needs to pull them out, not push them in.

According to Luke, Jesus started his ministry by declaring that he had arrived to pull the captives out. This was after his temptation in the desert, however. Jesus was tempted by the devil, who exercised the spiritual pressure of "pushiness." He tried to push Jesus to turn a stone into bread. He tried to push Jesus to his knees to worship him. He even tried to push Jesus off a cliff. It's fairly evident that, spiritually speaking, one team pushes while the other team pulls. After overcoming these temptations, Jesus declared that he is the Messiah who will pull us into freedom.

He came to Nazareth where he had been raised.
As he always did on the Sabbath, he went to
the meeting place. When he stood up to read,
he was handed the scroll of the prophet Isaiah.
Unrolling the scroll, he found the place where
it was written,

God's Spirit is on me;
    he's chosen me to preach the Message of good
        news to the poor,
Sent me to announce pardon to prisoners and
    recovery of sight to the blind,
To set the burdened and battered free,
    to announce, "This is God's time to shine!"

He rolled up the scroll, handed it back to the
assistant, and sat down. Every eye in the place was

on him, intent. Then he started in, "You've just
heard Scripture make history. It came true just now
in this place."

LUKE 4:16-21, MSG

It would behoove us to remember that everyone is already
captive to a habit, ideology, or religion. We may have been
trained to pressure people toward asking God for forgiveness, but that's not necessarily where people are when they
first encounter the gospel. Their response may well be:
"Forgiveness for what?" And in any case, the opportunity to
ask for forgiveness is itself not "good news," which is what
gospel signifies.

The offer of freedom from captivity is good news; the forgiveness of sin is the means of our redemption—the way that
we are delivered from our captivity. In that respect, forgiveness is too small a thing. God wants *repentance*, which means
going in a different direction. We *repent* of the way we've
been going in order to follow Jesus in the way he's leading.
Jesus then leads us through the forgiveness of our sin based
on his death on our behalf, and we find ourselves no longer
captive but living in freedom.

What if we reframed the question: "How does the Good
News of Jesus free this person from the pressures they feel in
a particular area of life?" For the business professional who
feels the shattering pressure to climb the corporate ladder,
Jesus declares that the highest status in the Kingdom is servant. For the Instagram model who lives and dies on the

altar of likes and followers, Jesus exemplifies the life of a world changer who had but a few followers. For the atheist materialist who only believes in what can be proven, Jesus offers tangible realities for ideas like love and justice.

People will follow whoever leads them to freedom. The goal is to see people follow Jesus, not ask for forgiveness.

I disagree with you.

It's an unfortunate confession: Christians are known more for what we are against than what we are for. It doesn't even take a personal relationship with a Christian for a nonbeliever to figure out that Facebook posts and protest signs are a badge of honor for so many of us in the Christian community. The spiritual gift of soapboxing. It is part of our diet, and it's not a hopeful message.

There is a strange impulse we have when talking with someone who is practicing something we don't agree with. Before the conversation ends, we feel the need to qualify our conversation by letting them know that we disagree with premarital sex (if premarital sex is the thing they are doing). Sometimes it's letting the nice gay couple next door know that we disagree with same-sex marriage. One time, I told my coffee-shop barista that I didn't agree with smoking marijuana. Since he brought it up.

There is a time and a place to speak about the negative consequences of truly destructive behaviors. And it is certainly the case that Jesus was known for both what he was for and what he was against. Even so, Jesus mostly spoke of what he was for when speaking to the nonreligious, and he spoke of what he was against when speaking to the religious. To this point, we must also remember that disagreement is a normal, natural part of any relationship. It's important to have a few safeguards in place so we realize we are at a healthy relational stage to have an honest discussion about a particular heated topic. Here are four questions to ask yourself before entering an intentional disagreement:

1. *If I am wrong on this issue, would I be willing to admit it?* If we aren't even willing to admit we are wrong, we aren't going to truly listen. Pursuing truth together means there is a humility (on both sides) to submit and admit. Submit to the truth, and admit when we didn't have it.

2. *Is this a head or a heart issue to the person I'm talking to?* If the issue is highly personal (heart), we need to spend more time acknowledging the emotions behind certain experiences. We need to keep reminding ourselves that Christianity is a religion built on the testimony of eyewitnesses allowed to voice their experiences. If you choose to believe the Gospels, you must choose to believe the accounts of those hurt by the church. Firsthand experiences are the name of the game.

3. *What is the desired outcome of this conversation?* If the purpose of the disagreement is to prove the other

person wrong, don't enter the conversation. Instead, we should see every disagreement as an opportunity to grow. For the aggressive personality, you can listen where you would normally speak up. And for the passive personality, you can speak up where you would be tempted to only listen. When your growth is the desired outcome of a disagreement, both participants will end up growing in the process.

4. *Will I be committed to the cleanup if this disagreement causes a mess?* Anyone can light a fuse. Not everyone has the commitment to rebuild when the bomb goes off. Misinterpretations of what was said happen. Saying the wrong thing when things get heated is common practice. Although these are things we try to avoid, the reality is that they are sometimes unavoidable, which is why this question is a necessary safeguard. If the disagreement causes a mess, are you committed to more conversations in order to rebuild the trust that may have been broken?

Even with those four questions as safeguards, let's not forget that sometimes our stance on issues is stronger than the Bible's. Years ago, I heard a well-known pastor refer to these as "personal legalisms." Look at the pseudoholy comments of any social-media post and you will quickly see what overzealous personal legalisms look like. When things we abstain from doing become the greatest identifier of who we are, it is difficult for people to see the One who is for them.

Enter the voting booth.

There can never be a distinctly Christian political position. Political positions are based on superiority, and disciples of Jesus are called to pursue humility. The attitudes of Christians are to be entirely different than, say, the attitudes of a political party. Christians are to regard themselves as lower than others (Philippians 2:3-5) and our sins as greater than others' (Matthew 7:1-3). Each kingdom of this world will always try to advance at the cost of those who are "less knowledgeable." *They just don't get it,* we tell ourselves. The echo chamber of our friend groups reinforces our perspectives, and before we know it, we are equating our constitutional rights with the way God intended things to be. Sure, we should vote wisely. But we should never label our party as "Christian."

In 2014, my friend Gregory Boyd was interviewed about his stance on politics. When asked about how Christians should vote, he said:

> Expressing an opinion about what government should do once every couple of years is a "token" way to care for the widow, orphan, poor and everyone else. People do their "civic duty" and can go back to their comfortable lives feeling good that they've "cared for" these folks because they had an opinion about how Caesar should care for these folks. I'm obviously not saying that all voters live this way, but the illusion that voting is the primary way to care

for the needy easily falls into this trap. The distinct kingdom way of caring for the widow, orphan, poor, oppressed, imprisoned, etc. . . . is to *actually* care for them, which means we *do something* to help them. We sacrifice of our lives, time and resources to make a difference, and in this way the glory goes to Christ rather than to Caesar, which should be our only concern.[5]

Something feels toxic when our moral convictions can be boiled down to red or blue. If you are going to be red, let it be because you have bled for your enemies. And if you are going to be blue, let it be because you have sat in sorrow with people who are experiencing pain. The Kingdom of God is holy. Meaning, it is set apart. It is other.

Thanks for asking.

Everyone knows someone who knows everything. At least, they think they know everything. One of the most annoying features about a know-it-all is the certainty by which they give answers to someone else's existential questions. Believe it or not, there are people out there who claim to know the answers to someone else's deepest questions about life. A Danish scientist by the name of Piet Hein put it like this: "Those who always know what's best are a universal pest."[6] And if you read that quote and are thinking, *What makes Pete the expert? I know better than that guy!*, chances are, you are that guy. Don't worry; this section should be helpful.

Why should uncertainty make us uncomfortable? The Bible frequently uses words like *mysteries* and *faith*. It is a conviction of Scripture that God's people would commit to a course of action in the face of uncertainty. We don't skirt around it, we run straight into it. Hebrews 11:1 tells us, "Faith is confidence in what we hope for and assurance about what we do not see" (NIV). Faith is anchored in confidence, not certainty. From all the criticism I have received over the years for hosting and training Doubters' Clubs, it is my belief that the opposite of faith is not doubt. The opposite of faith is certainty. And we have a steady diet of certainty-seeking faith that others find repulsive.

In the introduction to his book *Jesus Is the Question*, Martin Copenhaver cites two published studies that point out Jesus' answer-to-question ratio is 1:100.[7] For every answer Jesus gives, the Gospels record that he asks a hundred questions. Whatever his reasons were, it was not for a lack of knowledge. At age twelve, Jesus was keeping up with the Pharisees of his day. When Jesus chose to answer a question with a question, he modeled lovely responses of gentleness and concern for the questioner. Acting like Christ means there is no room to act like a know-it-all, even if you have the answer. By our own undoing, we will become saints of certainty that love giving simplistic, or reductionistic, answers to the mysteries of God—not only toward people but toward God himself. Let curiosity lead the way. Most people pursue what they are curious about. That's why they are entertaining questions in the first place.

Getting the Impression Right

The impression Jesus gave was attractive to the unbeliever, but will it always be that way? What about when Jesus returns to rid this world of all those who refuse to bow a knee? In his 2006 book, *Letter to a Christian Nation*, atheist Sam Harris wrote the following in his Note to the Reader:

Forty-four percent of the American population is convinced that Jesus will return to judge the living and the dead *sometime in the next fifty years.* According to the most common interpretation of biblical prophecy, Jesus will return only after things have gone horribly awry here on earth. It is, therefore, not an exaggeration to say that if the city of New York were suddenly replaced by a ball of fire, some significant percentage of the American population would see a silver lining in the subsequent mushroom cloud, as it would suggest to them that the best thing that is ever going to happen was about to happen: the return of Christ. It should be blindingly obvious that beliefs of this sort will do little to help us create a durable future for ourselves—socially, economically, environmentally, or geopolitically. Imagine the consequences if any significant component of the U.S. government actually believed that the world was about to end and that its ending would be *glorious.* The fact that nearly half of the American population apparently believes this, purely on the basis of religious dogma, should be considered a moral and intellectual emergency.[8]

On one hand, Harris has vastly mischaracterized the doctrine of the Second Coming. On the other hand, this is the impression he, and many others, have. To that note, I would say that this should be considered a moral emergency! Looking back at Christ's response to questioners and doubters is helpful inasmuch as we don't change tunes based on a false narrative about his return. For those who think Jesus will return like a general, wiping away the unbelievers with blissful fury, they might be in danger of jeopardizing gentleness and care in the current moment with what will eventually "get the job done" in the end. A. W. Tozer was right: "What comes into our minds when we think about God is the most important thing about us."[9] Take the "war passage" of Revelation as a case study.

I saw heaven standing open and there before me was a white horse, whose rider is called Faithful and True. With justice he judges and wages war. His eyes are like blazing fire, and on his head are many crowns. He has a name written on him that no one knows but he himself. He is dressed in a robe dipped in blood, and his name is the Word of God.

The armies of heaven were following him, riding
on white horses and dressed in fine linen, white
and clean.

REVELATION 19:11-14, NIV

Let's not miss a significant detail: Jesus has blood on his
robe before he rides into battle. To this point, N. T. Wright
points out that "the actual weapons which Jesus uses to win
the battle are his own blood, his loving self-sacrifice."[10] John,
the Revelator, gives us the impression that Jesus wins not
by the amount of people he can kill but by the amount of
people he has died for. The blood on his robe is his own! Till
the end, it is the blood of the Lamb that brings victory. The
story of the church starts by the self-sacrifice of Christ, and
it ends by the same token. Meaning: If we, the church, are
not willing to bleed for the one we disagree with, we should
not expect to win them over.

When it comes to people having the right impression of
you, everything is about acting like Jesus. If you are like me,
there is probably an impression that you need to rebuild.
Here is how you know: Someone thinks about Jesus in an
unfavorable way because of the way you reacted when you
disagreed with their action or confession.

I haven't gotten this right every time. My fifteen-year-old
self reacted to Cameron, giving him the impression that Jesus
would walk out on him if he openly admitted he was gay.

Here are some steps we can take, together, to rebuild the
impression people have of us:

1. *Apologize where you missed it.* Ask your nonreligious friend how they experienced you during that moment. We are all likely to continue showing up in the world the same way until we are told how people are experiencing us. Plus, if you have experienced an apology from someone in your life, you would agree that apologizing is the Miracle-Gro for any relationship. In 1 Corinthians 15:9, Paul says that he is "the least of the apostles." In Ephesians 3:8, he admits that he is "the very least of all the saints." In 1 Timothy 1:15, he confesses to being the "foremost" of sinners. In whatever month and year it is in your life, you can admit to misrepresenting Jesus in your moment of disappointment.

2. *Appreciate the journey they are on.* Have you ever felt what it is like to be appreciated by someone who disagrees with you? Not a backhanded compliment. I'm talking about a compliment when you were expecting to be backhanded. A word, or a gesture, that made you feel like you had worth regardless of your dissent. It's like telling the person from the opposite political party to make sure they vote and make their voice heard. And therein lies the key—helping people feel their worth. Decisions and worldviews aren't made in a vacuum. They have all sorts of stories and influences wrapped up in them. You don't have to agree with someone to appreciate the journey they are on.

3. *Anticipate that it's a long road ahead.* People who are committed to the friend in front of them will find themselves more satisfied, over time, with the relationship. I'll be the first to admit that this isn't efficient. It takes time and commitment, the two enemies of efficiency and scalability. Be that as it may, I am convinced that every negative impression of Jesus that I am responsible for was because I didn't see myself serving the person in front of me in the long term. On the other hand, every positive impression of Jesus that I am responsible for was because their impression of Jesus grew as I grew in Christ. We can't do this with everyone, but that was never the point. Pick one or two people in your life who aren't like you, and commit to them just as Christ committed to you before you were saved.

I Don't Wear Designer Clothes

The good news for all Christians is that bad impressions are redeemable. We may not get it right every time. In fact, we haven't gotten it right every time. There are ways we can redeem those bad impressions, however!

Working in a Christian organization and planting churches across the nation, I have my fair share of Christian clothing. Don't get me wrong; I always appreciate free stuff. But you won't catch me outside my house wearing Designer clothes—by which I mean clothing that markets God, the

Designer of it all. Shirts that have trite statements meant to remind the person passing by that Jesus loves them. Or that he is my homeboy (whatever that means).

My reasons for not wearing shirts like this revolves around the impression someone may have of God and the church. The person who already follows Jesus doesn't need my hoodie to remind them that Jesus is King. It's the person who doesn't follow Jesus that I am concerned about: the doubters and skeptics who have a terrible impression of Jesus and the church.

When the Doubters' Club team was designing a shirt for people who considered themselves part of the community, the back originally said, "Christians, atheists, and friends."

"Why is the word Christian first?" one of my coworkers asked. "If the community exists for those who doubt, you should put atheists first. Shouldn't it say, "Atheists, Christians, and friends"? You want them to have the right impression of everything you do!"

I called the T-shirt printer right away and told them we need to change the order of the words on the back.

"Why?" they asked.

"Because we want the doubters to have the right impression of everything we do!"

5

INTENTION

How to Renovate Your Intentions for the Nonbeliever

*Actually, most of the evil in this world is done by and through
"good" intentions. The cause of evil is stupidity, not malice.*

AYN RAND

*Elphie, now that we're friends,
I've decided to make you my new project.*

GLINDA, *Wicked the Musical*

WHEN I POSTED ABOUT OUR first Doubters' Club meeting
in Springfield, Missouri, I didn't anticipate the suspicion
people would have about it. I was part of the Springfield
Freethinkers Facebook group. I never participated in the discussions but always wanted to know how people in the city
viewed religion. People who don't view it as essential, that
is. The "misfits of the Midwest," you might call them. In
preparation for our first Doubters' Club meeting, I asked the
lead organizer of the Freethinkers' page if I could post about
the upcoming event.

"Sure," he replied. "As long as you aren't promoting a church service or anything of the sort." I get it. It was a Sunday morning before church when I posted it, and Sundays are holy days here in the Bible Belt.

A fairly basic invitation: "Atheist and Christian becoming better friends over coffee. Come join the conversation, model friendship, and pursue truth together." Along with the location details, there wasn't much else to it. I remember loading my kids into the van to get to church on time, and my phone was buzzing with nonstop notifications. I ignored it, thinking it was a group text that I was unknowingly looped into. But it didn't stop buzzing.

"Everyone buckled?" I was half paying attention when I asked the question. I figured I would use the time it took for the kids to get situated to check my messages. However, it wasn't a group text message. And my email notifications are always turned off. This time, it was my Facebook app that was blowing up with comments. Comments on the invitation post to our first meeting. Comments like the following:

"I just looked at your profile, and I see that you are a Christian. You're just trying to convert us! Almost fooled me. NOBODY GO!"

"Sorry, but I am suspicious of any Christian who puts together an event. I have never seen an event with Christians at it when they weren't trying to evangelize."

"Who let this joker in our group?"

And then a few more that wouldn't be appropriate to print in this publication. I drove to church feeling low-spirited by the reservation these people had of our intentions. I worshiped that morning with a pit in my stomach. The whole idea was disturbing to me. There was no arguing with them, either. Who was I to tell them that Christians can gather without proselytizing? Would I even be right in saying that? Jesus, on the other hand—he did it well. He wasn't just the life of the party; he brought the party to life.

Where have we gone wrong? I thought to myself. Unfortunately, I continued thinking to myself. *Is every event really a Trojan horse to turn them into one of us? Are we unable to have genuine relationships with nonbelievers? What would happen if we faced up to what drives us? Does anyone in the church know this is a problem?*

The service ended with my pastor inviting us to sign up for small groups. The pitch from the stage was that it was a place where unbelievers could feel welcome and build community so they could eventually hear the gospel. That's when it hit me. Somewhere between the end of service and picking my kids up from children's church, I realized that my annoyed, freethinking Facebook antagonists were right.

We don't really gather without trying to convert.

The Platinum Rule

Let me introduce you to Sarah. Sarah is an exemplary model of who the Doubters' Club exists for. True to type, she dresses to match her complexity of thought. Her version of a power suit would be luxury fabrics made of playful designs, a T-shirt with an abstract word or two under the neckline, and shoes that complement her mood, not her attire. She isn't concerned about climbing the ladder of success. Sarah wants to burn the ladder to the ground. Deconstruct the American dream and rebel against the status quo. When you talk to her, you will quickly find that high-spirited individualism is her business. She is a counselor who focuses on the endangered young adult. By her own admission, she wants to create safe spaces for people to become who they want to be, and it starts with removing barriers of unhealthy environments and habits. So naturally, I was surprised when she spoke up at her first meeting to critique the Golden Rule.

Her legs were crossed as she bounced one foot, noticeably. She had a thought loaded in the barrel. "When it comes to issues that we disagree on, I do not think we should live by the Golden Rule. The whole 'do unto others as you would have them do unto you' isn't always good."

I was shocked. This was the first time I had ever heard anyone disagree with these words of Jesus. It's common for people to disagree with the Bible. A little less common for them to disagree with the morals of Jesus. And as scarce as hen's teeth for someone to disapprove of Matthew 7:12.

"Do you think there is a better rule of thumb to live by?" I asked, tongue in cheek.

"Actually, I do. I heard this about twenty years ago, so it's not original to me. Someone once told me about the Platinum Rule."

"What's the Platinum Rule?" another asked. Even skeptics are curious how someone can one-up Jesus.

"Do unto others as they would have you do unto them," she replied. "How I want someone to treat me is not always how they want to be treated. If I learn to listen to them first, I can treat them how they want to be treated. For example, Christians evangelize because if they were lost and going to hell, they would want someone to tell them about Jesus. Therefore, they feel that, according to the Golden Rule, they should be telling others about Jesus."

I'll admit that I was disoriented. On the one hand, it's tragic when people dismiss the significance of what Jesus says in the Gospels. On the other hand, it pains me to say that, in relation to her specific example, she had a point. Sarah was getting at the negative form of the Golden Rule. When the rule is put in its negative form, we need to refrain from doing unto others what they would not have us do unto them. This would seem like common sense to a counselor like her, or to anyone who wants to help the person in front of them. It's the positive form of the rule that she didn't understand. Scottish author William Barclay writes about Jesus' words here when he says:

> The only man who can even begin to satisfy the positive form of the rule is the man who has the love of Christ within his heart. He will try to forgive as he would wish to be forgiven, to help as he would wish to be helped, to praise as he would wish to

be praised, to understand as he would wish to be understood. He will never seek to avoid doing things; he will always look for things to do.[1]

We call it the Golden Rule because in AD 222–35, Roman Emperor Alexander Severus was so impressed with how comprehensive this maxim was that he had it inscribed in gold on the walls of his chamber.[2] Since then, we have been inscribing it on pillows, putting it on bumper stickers, and proudly teaching it to our children. It might be losing its impressiveness with the skeptic, however. The Golden Rule is only impressive if it is acted out genuinely. And when we befriend people for the sake of saving them, we are being anything but genuine.

When it comes to building lasting friendships, we Christians haven't always been able to do this without untold intentions. One of my mentors in seminary, David Leatherberry, wrote a book titled *Abdul and Mr. Friday*. It is the true story of a Christian's lifelong friendship with a Muslim. Abdul and Mr. Friday both resolved to remain good friends even though they believed different things. It wasn't that they didn't want to see the other believe like them; their friendship just wasn't based on whether that happened. In fact, the subtitle of David's book made that clear: "Neither Wanted to Go to Heaven Without the Other." They were genuine with one another about their hopes for each other, and their friendship was one of the most impressive ones I have seen. After twenty-five years of not believing Jesus was who the Christian said he was, "Abdul" was still being visited by "Mr. Friday," even if it required a flight across the world to see him.

Relationships with nonbelievers can become incredibly formative. They will chip away at the disingenuousness, causing us to become more secure in who God is forming us to be. They will also baptize the mind with fuller and deeper understandings of the truths that can only be known through studying a book or person.

Weak at the Knees (Becoming Genuine)

Superman hasn't always had the power of flight. When he was first created, he had the ability to leap tall buildings in a single bound. A magnificent power, but it wasn't flight. It wasn't until the 1940s that animators decided to give him this new superpower. Animators at the time felt that it would be too cumbersome to draw him routinely bending his knees when landing. Instead, they told everyone that he could fly. It was a new law of physics for the cartoon world: What goes up doesn't have to come down. It helped make the animation smooth, which was easier on readers. It's always easier to gain a superpower than to expose a weakness, but the long-term effects of this decision to make Superman fly are still playing out.

In his book *I Don't Want to Talk About It*, Terrence Real writes about how men can overcome the secret legacy of male depression. He diagnoses depression as a "disorder of feeling" that causes many men to hide their weaknesses and vulnerabilities.[3] It is a barrier to showing up as genuine in the world. Real writes:

> For generations, we have chosen male heroes who literally are not made of vulnerable flesh— Superman, "the man of steel." . . . And our love of invulnerability shows little sign of abating. Both celebrities and ordinary men across the country have developed a new fascination with muscle.[4]

Real writes about depression specifically, but the "let's not be vulnerable" narrative of Superman applies to all of us. It takes too much time to show where we are weak at the knees. Let's assume a superpower when sharing our stories, so the listener is impressed. All the while, we are becoming more disingenuous. Not to mention how difficult it must be for our nonbelieving friends to identify with us. Our superpowers make us super unapproachable.

It's worth mentioning here that Terrence Real's book isn't explicitly Christian. Our nonbelieving friends are equally vulnerable to presenting themselves as invulnerable. The most basic thing that connects us to nonbelievers is that they, like we, are fully human. Apparently, the mystic poet Thomas Merton was right when he described himself as "a member of a human race which is no more (and no less) ridiculous than I am myself."[5]

If you are to become more genuine, *avoid generalizations*

about your life and share specifics. Instead of "we all struggle," how about you share about yesterday and the day before that? How you've had trouble showing up to work on time. How your marriage has a valley called "anger" that you seem to be walking through with your spouse. How you have doubted God's goodness after being diagnosed with cancer. As John Wesley said, "Let your words be the genuine picture of your heart."[6]

Another step toward the right side of the scale is to *share stories where the other person is the hero.* Instead of lending a helping hand and being the hero in your story, lend someone your shoulders. Lift them up! Make them better. Be generous with your encouragement. Exaggerate their success and minimize their failure. Proverbs 27:2 says, "Don't brag about yourself—let others praise you" (CEV). Be the other who is praising them! The most genuine person in the room knows how to make a hero out of the most forgotten in the room. This was the point in many of Jesus' parables!

- The Good Samaritan (Luke 10:25-37)
- The praying tax collector in the temple (Luke 18:9-14)
- The Prodigal Son (Luke 15:11-32)

Finally, *genuine people are sought after because they are trustworthy.* They are rarely spreading gossip disguised as emails to the leader of the church's prayer chain. They don't share details of another person's life because they treasure that person too much to have others think poorly of them.

Put simply, they genuinely care about the person. They are so aware of their own deficiencies that they consider the struggles of the unbeliever to be but a speck in their eye (Matthew 7:1-5). The doubts and disbelief of their neighbors aren't what identifies genuine people.

Gardens, Not Factories

I like listening to people who know what they are talking about. It becomes impressive, though, when they know who they are talking to. Jesus shared a parable about how his disciples should think about sharing their knowledge of the Kingdom of God: "the knowledge of the secrets of the kingdom of heaven has been given to you" (Matthew 13:11, NIV). I'm referring to the parable of the soils, found in the three synoptic Gospels (Matthew, Mark, and Luke).

It's the story of a farmer who is willing and ready to sow seed into the ground. The farmer casts the seed, indiscriminately, on four types of soil. It's here that we wonder if each soil represents a different state of the heart. Not to be dogmatic, but we have to handle parables carefully. They are not meant to be allegorical; each detail is not representative of a greater truth. Otherwise, we would be infusing made-up stories with our own subjective agendas. Rather, I agree with Bible commentator Adolf Jülicher that parables have a single point, and the rest is narrative scenery.[7] This approach to interpreting parables helps us focus on Jesus' heart and character without being deterred by details. Whether the soils represent seasons of a person's life or the status of their heart, I'm not sure. What I am confident about is the most important truth: Jesus wants us to understand the human heart as soil and think of it the way a farmer might. On the contrary, the modern era, with its emphasis on efficiency and repetition, has led us to view even discipleship through a lens of the factory model. But people are gardens, not factories.

If people are gardens, knowledge should be treated like the seeds that will, eventually, grow. We need to make sure that the seeds we are planting will produce something of the Kingdom when fully grown. And you can't rush it. Some questions need to be revisited for years before the answer takes. Some answers need to be revisited for years for a good question to take.

Sometimes we have to make sure it's not a faulty seed. "If it's not good news, then it's not the gospel" is a common saying at the Doubters' Club. Some seeds should never have been planted. You must keep growing in the knowledge and truth that comes from seeking answers to your friend's questions to make sure that you are casting the right seed. I am deeply concerned that Christians stop growing out of a multitude of reasons.

Too busy.

Too bored.

Heard it too many times.

Whatever your reason may have been, never stop learning "to grasp how wide and long and high and deep is the love of Christ" (Ephesians 3:18, NIV). Otherwise, you will spend a lot of time trying to grow a seed that produces "twice as much a son of hell as you are" (Matthew 23:15, AMP).

> [Jesus said,] "You're hopeless, you religion scholars
> and Pharisees! Frauds! You go halfway around
> the world to make a convert, but once you get
> him you make him into a replica of yourselves,
> double-damned."
> MATTHEW 23:15, MSG

When to Close the Deal

"Am I allowed to talk? Do you want me to say anything?" Pastor Scott was the pastor of our sending church back when we were church planting. He came all the way from Texas to Denver to spend time with my family and check out a Doubters' Club meeting.

"Of course you can!" I said. "Say whatever you want. We usually don't quote Scripture because a lot of people there don't believe in the Bible."

"I totally get it," he said with his animated personality. I could tell he was excited to participate.

This particular meeting was taking place at our downtown Denver location. We usually packed around twenty people in the lower half of the café, making just enough room for our drinks on the tables. After welcoming everyone, we went over the rules and started discussing the topic they voted on the time before. Questions about the reliability of the Bible quickly came up. Honestly, I can't remember if that was the topic of choice or if the conversation led us there. Either way, it was the back-and-forth for a good portion of the meeting.

When the meeting ended, we had exactly thirty-five minutes to get to church for our Sunday evening service, and it was a thirteen-minute drive. Scott, his son, and I tried to give the friendliest, rushed good-bye before jumping in his truck, with me at the wheel.

"Preston, I have a question."

"Sure, Pastor Scott. What's up?" I have trouble driving and talking at the same time, but we were still getting out of the parking garage at this point.

"I know you knew the answers to those questions. You and I have talked about that topic before. You could have blown them away if you wanted to. Why did you hold back?" One of the most endearing qualities about Pastor Scott is that he believes he can learn from anyone in the room. Or the truck.

"The intention of the Doubters' Club is not to 'win' the debate," I told him. "The intention is to build a platform of friendship for us to pursue truth together." I shared with him that we do not intend to ever pray the prayer of salvation at a Doubters' Club meeting. Our intention is to build friendships with people who don't think like us. The common ground we all have is our doubts.

This story has become a great memory for Pastor Scott and me. One of the most memorable truck rides of my life.

When he shares the story, he always speaks so highly of the interactions he witnessed that day at that little coffee shop in Denver. I count it a compliment to hear him share about it. Yet, I realized that day that he is one of the most genuine and impressive people I know.

His intention as a mega-church pastor was never to convert me to one. In fact, while I was pastoring our church plant, it never grew past 130 attendees. He never intruded on the ways we did church (although sometimes he should have). His only intention was understanding the story God was writing through our family in Denver. He asked questions, led tenderly, and we laughed together a whole lot. He gained more trust and influence than he would have any other way.

The purer the intentions, the more influence we gain.

Every. Single. Time.

6

INVITATION

How to Invite the Nonbeliever into Real Life, Not a Church Service

You can make more friends in two months
by becoming interested in other people than you can
in two years by trying to get other people interested in you.
DALE CARNEGIE, *How to Win Friends and Influence People*

I have an enormous amount of trouble getting people
to come to my place. . . . I can't tell you how much
leftover guacamole I've eaten.
MICHAEL SCOTT, *The Office*

IN A DEVOTIONAL ON THE POWER OF GRACE, Charles Swindoll tells this story.

During his days as president, Thomas Jefferson and a group of companions were traveling across the country on horseback. They came to a river which had left its banks because of a recent downpour. The swollen river had washed the bridge away. Each rider

was forced to ford the river on horseback, fighting
for his life against the rapid currents. The very real
possibility of death threatened each rider, which
caused a traveler who was not part of their group
to step aside and watch. After several had plunged
in and made it to the other side, the stranger asked
President Jefferson if he would ferry him across the
river. The president agreed without hesitation. The
man climbed on, and shortly thereafter the two of
them made it safely to the other side. As the stranger
slid off the back of the saddle onto dry ground,
one in the group asked him, "Tell me, why did you
select the president to ask this favor of?" The man
was shocked, admitting he had no idea it was the
president who had helped him. "All I know," he said,
"is that on some of your faces was written the answer
'No,' and on some of them was the answer 'Yes.' His
was a 'Yes' face."[1]

We are all travelers bound to face storms, rivers, and the
nasty mess that happens when the two combine. The dis-
orientation that occurs when your teenage daughter calls to
tell you she's pregnant. The trauma of cancer winning when
the person still had so much more life to live. The reality
of betrayal as the company that you built starts to fall. The
divorce. The lies. The religion. The bankruptcy. We approach
the situation and quickly realize that the banks have become
blurry as the storm refuses to cease.

Where do we start?
When will it end?
How do we cross?

"The storms will come," Jesus said. "And when they do, climb aboard. No one crosses alone." My paraphrase, but you get the idea. Over two thousand years ago, Jesus put on his "yes" face. He invited us to hold on to what C. S. Lewis calls the "hope of our eternal country."[2] Jesus is the "yes" face of God, always inviting us into his life and requesting that we invite him into ours. Eugene Peterson captured the essence of this when he translated John 16:33 in *The Message*:

[Jesus said,] "I've told you all this so that trusting me, you will be unshakable and assured, deeply at peace. In this godless world you will continue to experience difficulties. But take heart! I've conquered the world."

For people who don't yet have Jesus, they have us. Is there room on the back of your saddle for a weary traveler who needs safe passage? Christian or not, everyone is journeying a similar path. The difference is not in what we experience along the way; the difference is in who is committed to the journey with us. If you take this seriously, the day is coming when your unbelieving friend will look at you, shocked and a little embarrassed, and say, "All I know is that when the rest of the world had a 'No' face, yours said 'Yes.'"

It was all because you chose to have on your "Yes" face.

You were like Jesus to them.

Inviting them into your life and committing to the crossing.

Haircuts, Cheesy Pretzels, and Genuine Conversations

My barber, Jeremy, was never going to go to church. He was a bisexual swinger dating a man. He had a hole in his ear, just big enough to hold his cigarette while he gave me a number-2 cut on the sides and half an inch off the top. More potent than the smell of the burning cigarette was the smell of whiskey. Jeremy wasn't always sober when he gave me haircuts, but it didn't seem to affect his job. Cigarettes, whiskey, and tattoos. Lots of tattoos. A vulgar, scornful phrase was tattooed onto his eyelids. On the slight chance that you did get him to church, you may not want him to bow his head and close his eyes. He was the opposite of all the pictures you see on most churches' social media. His look wasn't traditional, and his theology wasn't exclusive. To make things worse, he grew up in the church. That is, until they kicked his mom out for being a lesbian. It wasn't just that Jeremy didn't have a chance in the church; the church was *unwilling to give Jeremy a chance.*

He had experienced church many times over again, and it seemed to be the same thing. The church would put their best foot forward through an invitation to their service and then refuse to use the other foot to walk with him. Church was in the past for him. He didn't have time for people with ulterior motives. He had an eagerness to learn about his client's lives. The name of my wife, kids, and favorite coffee at the local coffee shop next door. Before I knew it, I was asking questions back to him.

"How's your daughter?" Who would have known he had a daughter?

"How are you losing so much weight?" I had no idea he was self-conscience about his body.

"How's the big move going?" We had to move too. It got too expensive in the city.

I have daughters. I was trying to lose weight. We were moving. Jeremy and I had a lot more in common than what meets the eye.

"Preston, how is the Doubters' Club going?" It was typical for him to ask about the times and location of our meetings.

"Going well, Jeremy. You know . . ." I had to be careful not to make him feel like I was inviting him to a service. "The Doubters' Club exists for you, but you don't have to ever show up. I consider these haircuts to be like our own Doubters' Club meetings." In my enthusiasm, I still had to have discretion.

Jeremy paused. The clippers kept running, but he was holding them away from my head. I could tell he was thinking.

"What do you think about my lifestyle?" It's the game-over question for so many in the LGBTQ+ community. "Is the church you're starting accepting of people like me?"

"Jeremy . . . I hope that you see my intention is not to get you to church. I love having you as a friend and would like to hear more of your story." I wasn't avoiding the issue. I just knew that talking about emotionally charged topics, without a strong friendship, can (and oftentimes does) result in disaster.

"Well," he thought about it. "At 2:00 p.m. on Wednesdays, I go to the pub next door and get a pretzel with cheese on my break. Wanna join?"

"Yes!" I couldn't wait to learn more about him. Every two to three weeks, I would sit in that barber chair, only to hear echoes of his life. Those echoes would fade away as the weeks went by. An invitation into real life is just what we needed for our friendship to grow legs and go somewhere.

We rarely missed a Wednesday. Through those times, I learned more about his past relationships, his experiences in the church, and his family. Sometimes we would sit and watch a game. Other times, we would talk about God and how confusing life can be. I remember one Wednesday when the rain was pouring for Jeremy, and he needed to hitch a ride across a deep, theological river.

"Can I ask you something, Preston?" He sipped the cheapest beer he could buy as we carefully approached a topic he was having trouble with.

"Of course."

"I don't know what I think about the afterlife. I know you have beliefs about God, heaven, hell, and all that. I don't know what your stance on all of that is. But I actually want my life to count for something. And if there is something after this life, I want to know."

With that question, we started journeying through C. S. Lewis's *The Great Divorce* together. It was a great way to explore questions about the afterlife without shoving Christian orthodoxy down his throat. In fact, it was Lewis's line, "You cannot love a fellow-creature fully till you love God," that helped Jeremy learn to love God above all else.[3]

Making It Personal

These sorts of questions are the natural progression of living the Doubters' Club as a lifestyle. Remember, it's not a thing we do. It's a new way to do everything! When you have someone invite you into their life, that invitation isn't just to pretzels and cheese. Or a drink. Or coffee. It's into life. The things they draw life from and the things that scare them to death. With time, vulnerability and trust become the norm. And it's not just on their part. If we are doing this as genuinely as possible, *we* start to change in the process. Committed friendships between nonbelievers and believers help us unlearn what it means to be churched and relearn what it means to be the church. Sometimes we find our beliefs changing—sometimes profoundly—but what always, inevitably changes is our hearts.

Invitations into life also allow the love and patience of Christ within us to greatly transform the stories in front of us. There are narratives that have since been forgotten by the church that are now being resurrected through you. I have seen it happen in Doubters' Club meetings and on the street where the most unlikely group of people talk about the most unlikely topics and end up having the most unlikely friendships.

Jeremy's story may stand out to you as unique, but I could also tell you about Sam. Sam was a Satanist who, years ago, had a baby with a stripper. Since then, he has had two more children with two different women. My kids were scared of the way Sam looked, and I was scared for the direction he was going. After months of attending Doubters' Club meetings, we started inviting one another to lunch. It became a monthly meeting. And then, one Thursday around noon, Sam told me that he had a peace that he had never experienced before. I asked him where that peace was coming from. We talked about how, if God were real, he would probably want his children to have peace. Sam started following Jesus that day.

At least a Satanist has some sort of spiritual curiosity. Some of the greatest friendships I have are with people who are certain that spirituality is a hoax. Like my friend Wesley.

Wesley has been the atheist co-host for many Doubters' Club meetings. Our friendship naturally progressed to hanging out and texting each other during our spare time. He even started attending the church we planted. As would be expected, he had lots of questions afterward. My favorite questions revolve around real life, not ethereal possibilities that only appeal to the upper echelon of people. Those people draw their life from being right. I want to talk with people like Wesley who draw life from their relationships. One night he asked me whether God would ever care about his success and future relationships. "Those are the things that matter to me," he told me. "If God is real, wouldn't he care about the things that I care about?" To this day, I don't know if Wesley is what you would consider a "Christian." What I do know is that we are both way closer to Jesus than we were when we first met.

Skeptics and agnostics will always invite you into their lives before they invite Jesus in. In previous chapters, we have talked through how the impression they have of you really does matter. A good impression comes from leading the way in what matters most to the person you are talking to. Namely, humility in our questions, vulnerability about our weaknesses, and repenting when we aren't true to our word.

After impression is intention. It's a soul check to see whether we have ulterior motives. Does my friendship with this person depend on them deciding to follow Christ within some allotted amount of time? (Ulterior motive.) Or do I intend to befriend this person and share my life with them, regardless of if they ever decide to become a follower of Christ? (Ultimate motive.) We all have ultimate motives. We should be fierce about getting rid of ulterior motives. Now let's discuss how to invite people into our lives and accept the invitation into theirs.

How to Invite People into a Life-Giving Relationship

1. Make seeing them a natural rhythm of your life.

Naturally, we all have our favorite restaurants, movie theaters, and neighbors. We are drawn to frequent the places and people that make us feel the most comfortable. Let's face it—it is uncomfortable to be uncomfortable. Add onto this our schedules. They seem to be bursting at the seams as we try to keep our commitments, make new commitments, answer when our family calls, make love to our spouse, play with the kids, catch up with the news, go to the gym, and keep up with a hobby. (My therapist keeps telling me I can't forget about having a hobby—a hobby that doesn't involve any of the above-said activities and obligations.) And now we are supposed to be intentional about connecting with people who don't think like we do? Does my mother-in-law count?

Oscar Wilde said, "Consistency is the last refuge of the unimaginative."[4] So stop getting up with just enough time to get to work. Get up at 5:06 a.m. Walk your dog. Take a new route home. Play rock, paper, scissors with your spouse to see who does the next chore. Rent a movie with subtitles. Read a children's book. Listen to a new genre of music. Read to the blind. Start counting the yellow cars that drive by. Subscribe to a start-up company's newsletter. Go canoeing at midnight. Don't picket your next cause; give pizza to the picketers. Call your crazy uncle. Teach some kid the thing you do best. Listen to someone talk for two hours. Take up swing dancing. Change your mind about something.

Get off the phone when you're ordering coffee. Learn someone's name. Make their name a treasure in your heart. Visit this person again. Say their name out loud. Tell them your favorite story. Ask them about their Peter Pan tattoo.

Get a pastry. Reschedule with your barber before you leave. Ask them what the craziest haircut they have ever given was. Look up when you walk into the coffee shop. Take your headphones out. Buy your barber a drink and introduce him to Lucy. Remember Lucy? The barista on the other side of the counter? Tell him about Lucy's tattoo and what it means to her. For God's sake, make your comfortable routines uncomfortable by getting to know the people who are usually serving you. Serve them simply by looking up, asking questions, smiling, and visiting them again. If Jesus came to serve and not be served, at some point we need to do the same.

Assuming you are trying to read through this chapter before your next meeting, *you do not necessarily need to add routines to your schedule*. What if you just became intentionally uncomfortable in your most comfortable environments? In an article entitled "Science Has Just Confirmed That If You're Not Outside Your Comfort Zone, You're Not Learning," *Inc.com* writer Jessica Stillman explains, "Stability shuts down your brain's learning centers, new Yale research shows."[5] As Yale neuroscientist Daeyeol Lee put it to *Quartz*, "Perhaps the most important insight from our study is that the function of the brain as well as the nature of learning is not 'fixed' but adapts according to the stability of the environment. . . . When you enter a more novel and volatile environment, this might enhance the tendency for the brain to absorb more information."[6] Five-time entrepreneur Auren Hoffman says that we should fill 70 percent of our schedules with tasks that stretch our capabilities.[7] Believe it or not, science and Jesus seem to agree on a lot more than we may think.

Jesus said no to adding to his schedule. "I've come for the lost sheep of Israel," he said, and he never deviated from that (Matthew 15:24, author's paraphrase). This is why he commissioned Paul to the Gentiles. However, in a typical Jewish-carpenter fashion, Jesus had routines. He had a close group of friends, a small circle of disciples, and shopped locally. His family mattered to him, but so did his church attendance. At a young age, he ditched his parents and was found teaching in the synagogue. Jesus knew what it meant to grow up in a religious bubble. Yet, he was the most learned rabbi those in the ancient Near East had ever seen. If we removed all the highly enculturated locations and relationships from Jesus' life, we would lose the Gospels entirely. So how did he do it? How did Jesus grow in his knowledge of God and people when his life revolved around people who worshiped God and places where God was worshiped?

Jesus was intentional about making comfortable environments uncomfortable for the sake of the person who didn't have a relationship with him.

When Jewish norms would have him look down on talking with a Samaritan woman, Jesus spoke to her with admiration and value. And he did so while traveling through Samaria (John 4:1-45).

Conventional Jewish practice would mean maximizing

on a relationship with a rich young ruler (this is true in many cultures today). In a very uncomfortable fashion, Jesus minimized the value of the man's dollar and told him to give it all away. This conversation happened "as [Jesus] was setting out on [a] journey" (Mark 10:17).

It was normal for crowds to surround Jesus with their needs. What was abnormal was that the Messiah gave attention to the one who slipped into his presence unnoticed, bleeding, and barely brave enough to touch his robe. This took place "when Jesus returned" from his travels (Luke 8:40).

On his way. As he was setting out. When he returned. These are all indicators that Jesus had natural rhythms of life. American philosopher Dallas Willard was asked to summarize Jesus in one word.

"Relaxed," he said.[8] Not busy. Not occupied with too much. Jesus was intentional. Everything was done on purpose.

Jesus was intentional about seeing people within his routines. He didn't overlook anyone. He saw them. If we are to see people like Jesus did, we must do what he did: Learn their names, learn their stories, and learn what they need.

Who is a person you normally see but don't know their name? Learn their name and write it here:

What is their story? Ask them where they are from. What brought them to the city you live in? What's the story behind their tattoos? What do they do in their free time? Once you know their story, write it here:

_____

_____

_____

What do they need? Did you pick up on the stress they feel at their job? Are they a student who is struggling to make ends meet? When you learn what they need, write it here:

_____

_____

_____

2. Ask to join a natural rhythm of their life.

My daughters are five and seven, and we don't think alike at all. At this point in their lives, they do not care about the things I care about. My seven-year-old loves crafts and dancing to the most recent Kidz Bop playlist, while my five-year-old wants to play Barbies upstairs. Imagine if all I did was invite them to go to the office with me. Or to do the dishes. Imagine if every day I invited my daughters to use their marker-stained hands to help me type out the words to this book. Not only would they not care, they would start to avoid me because all I would be doing is inviting them into my life. And my life is highly irrelevant to them. If I want to have a relationship with them, I need to be willing to arabesque and play Barbie DreamHouse.

Have you ever thought about how strange it must feel when unchurched people constantly get invited to church? It's probably equally bizarre when we tell them that we are praying for them. Like when your CFO tries to explain the monthly financial reports. I'm guessing it's maddening, to say the least. If we want to have a relationship with people who do not think like us, we have to love them enough to start where they are. I can't imagine Jesus was all that concerned with catching fish. I can't help but believe that he started there because that's what was important to his soon-to-be disciples.

The chief trait of this kind of living is *showing genuine interest in the person through showing interest in what the person is doing*. When we were starting our first Doubters' Club in Denver, my wife had a great idea to get to know some of the people at the coffee shop where the meetings were being held. She started making scones every Thursday and delivering them on Fridays to the shop. The owner could sell them to increase his profit for the weekend. Of course, she had to ask permission first. She noticed that selling pastries is a natural rhythm of life for the business. She asked permission to be a baker. And she learned to make delicious scones in the process.

What I am saying here is to make your agenda them, not you. It would be a paradigm shift for the church. The church is the only institution that exists 100 percent for the good of the people who do not consume the goods of the organization, however. When you ask someone if you can join their life, do so in a way that adds value to them—not you.

No to Church. Yes to You.

Comedian Steven Wright said, "There's a fine line between fishing and standing on the shore like an idiot." The Doubters' Club lifestyle is for people who are tired of looking like an idiot. Instead of just inviting people to a church service, we have to have intentional invitations that revolve around investing time into people's interests and needs. This is not a sexy way to do church. It makes no promise to grow Sunday attendance, and it requires more, not less, of you. But it is so worth it!

I must admit to you what I admit to all the Doubters' Club pioneers that I train. My hesitancy is that all this seems too difficult. It's uncomfortable, and it requires more of me than I am willing to give most days. *If this is the only life I have to live*, I often think, *then I must make the most of the days I have.* Since I started living Doubters' Club as a lifestyle, I started to be more and more convicted that this stage of invitation is more necessary than any of the other preceding *I*s mentioned in the book thus far. Yes, the impression people have is important. Yes, you must check your intentions if it's going to be a genuine friendship. In whatever way you practice the other two, you cannot skip the invitation. For you are not just inviting someone into your life, and they aren't just inviting you into theirs.

You are inviting them into the next life. Let them climb aboard, and help them cross the river. You both are going somewhere much bigger than yourselves!

7

INITIATION

How to Re-examine Our Views through Conversations That Matter

A good conversation can shift the direction of change forever.
LINDA LAMBERT

*"Still," he says, "if I shared my doubts with you, about God
and love and life and death, that's all you'd have: a bunch
of doubts. But now, see, you've got all these great jokes."*
DANIEL WALLACE, *Big Fish: A Novel of Mythical Proportions*

BACK IN DENVER, the Doubters' Club started out of an organic friendship. It emerged naturally over time and at the right time. Back in Denver, we stopped expecting one another to be perfect, and we liked each other for who we were: unbridled disruptors of the unexamined life who talked about our doubts and discomforts in a rather comforting way. That's a tall order to fill when starting a Doubters' Club anywhere else. Now I live in Springfield, Missouri: the buckle of the Bible Belt. After five months of living here, my wife affectionately stopped me in my tracks, looked me in the eyes, and said, "I know you are training Doubters' Club leaders around the world, but something dies in you when you are not leading one. I think your soul needs to be having conversations with doubters." With an equal degree of plainspokenness, she continued with "now help me do the dishes." Dishes first, then on to planning our first meeting.

It was our first time gathering as a group, and I wasn't convinced the conversation was going to go well. I knew some of the people attending. Others were invited through Facebook or the like. And yet eighteen people showed up to initiate a conversation that matters.

With people they don't know.

Trust.

Or agree with.

You could feel the stereotypes pinned to one another like shadows. Mere simpleminded outlines of who they really were, but still scary to the person who didn't know any better. There was the Christian hipster who held up the line by asking whether the coffee beans were single origin, with a noticeable tattoo of an archer's bow on his forearm. You don't have to know what it means to know it means something biblical. Then there was the gypsy agnostic with multicolored hair, an oat-milk latte, and sandals that looked more worn than the ancient Near Eastern rabbi that she didn't believe in. Atheists are rather self-identifying as well. Even though the Doubters' Club covers the tab, they will buy their own coffee, suspiciously seat themselves away from the front, and "talk less . . . smile more," as Aaron Burr puts it in *Hamilton*.[1] No strings attached. Don't sit close enough to get attached. And still try to have a good time.

My barber was the nonbeliever leading the conversation with me that day. We did our best to make everyone feel welcome. The question we opened with was: "Why did you decide to come to the meeting?" Usually we will talk about what the group voted on the time before. As was evident by the fiddling thumbs in the room, this was our first meeting. It was so awkward, people were sipping imaginary drinks from empty cups in order to avoid talking.

"I'll start." A voice from the back spoke up. He had long red hair, with a beard to match in every way. "My name's David. I saw the invitation online, and I came because I need to learn how to initiate conversations with my parents."

"So glad you are here, David. What makes it so difficult to talk with your parents?" I asked.

"They are Christians. The kind of Christians that believe I'm going to hell because I'm an atheist. It's gotten to the point that we don't even know how to have a conversation anymore about anything that matters. So I'm here to learn how to do that." Can you believe it? It's not always the parents who are rehearsing for the return of the prodigal. Sometimes, the prodigal is wondering how exactly they are supposed to come home.

The textbook answer to "What does David believe?" would be that he is an atheist. He doesn't believe in anything. However, it's never good to define someone by the textbook definition. More interesting than definitions are stories. It's the thing people are made of.

Others shared his sentiment. The gypsy girl couldn't remember the last time she had a meaningful conversation with her conservative mother from a small town in Missouri. I think her exact words were, "I would love to be able to talk with her for more than ten minutes." As the stereotype dimmed, we all realized that it wasn't just the soles of her sandals that were worn. Her vulnerable confession was significant to the group. It opened us all up to talking about the most thoughtful ways to initiate conversations that matter with those who don't think like us.

And that's what I want to talk with you about. How do you have a worthwhile conversation with someone who disagrees with the way you define them? Chances are, they want to talk with you, too!

Jesus and the Thirsty Woman

It's the longest recorded conversation he ever had. Well over ten minutes. And it was with someone whom some would say Jesus never should have met. First off, the person was a she, not a he. In the ancient Near East, the female gender was looked on as significantly lower in society. (For the record, I do not share that opinion.) Secondly, she wasn't a religious elite or a chosen disciple. She wasn't even one of the "common" folks who attended the wedding Jesus was at a few chapters earlier. Third, she was a Samaritan. As Franciscan author Pat McCloskey put it, "Imagine the hatred between Serbs and Muslims in modern Bosnia, the enmity between Catholics and Protestants in Northern Ireland or the feuding between street gangs in Los Angeles or New York, and you have some idea of the feeling and its causes between Jews and Samaritans in the time of Jesus. Both politics and religion were involved."[2] Did I mention it was the longest conversation he had?

> Now he had to go through Samaria. So he came to
> a town in Samaria called Sychar, near the plot of
> ground Jacob had given to his son Joseph. Jacob's
> well was there, and Jesus, tired as he was from the
> journey, sat down by the well. It was about noon.
> When a Samaritan woman came to draw water,
> Jesus said to her, "Will you give me a drink?" (His
> disciples had gone into the town to buy food.)
> The Samaritan woman said to him, "You are a
> Jew and I am a Samaritan woman. How can you
> ask me for a drink?" (For Jews do not associate
> with Samaritans.)
>
> JOHN 4:4-9, NIV

To say Jesus had to go through Samaria to get from Judea to Galilee is like American Airlines telling me I have to go through Dallas to get to New York City from Springfield. Sure, it is one of the routes. But it is most certainly not the only one. He was intentionally seeking a conversation with someone who would resist his in-group. Even the woman was shocked at his request for a drink. When I read this, I can't help but notice how the author, John, notes that the disciples (himself included) were away buying food when this encounter took place. It's as if he doesn't want to be blamed by his readers for the conversation Jesus is about to initiate.

At first Jesus sounds like an evangelist, offering mysterious living water, but he quickly also sounds like a prophet to the woman when he, a stranger, demonstrates that he knows intimate details of her life. As the conversation ensues, Jesus draws a parallel between her thirst and the living water that he gives. She acknowledges that both are true, but there's a problem. "Our ancestors worshiped on this mountain, but you Jews claim that the place where we must worship is in Jerusalem" (John 4:20, NIV). Remember when you invited your friend to church and your friend said, "I can never go to church. The building would probably fall or get struck by lightning the moment I walk in"? That's the kind of excuse we are dealing with. There may be a need, but it's not anything traditional religion would be interested in fixing.

Jesus forever changed the narrative around who can worship the Father. He pulls the final Jenga block from the theological tower that stood between her and the Man who would finally satisfy.

> Yet a time is coming and has now come when the
> true worshipers will worship the Father in the Spirit
> and in truth, for they are the kind of worshipers the

Father seeks. God is spirit, and his worshipers must
worship in the Spirit and in truth.

JOHN 4:23-24, NIV

The conversation closes with what I call the "sinner's non-
prayer." The religious thing to do would be to say, "Repeat
after me." Instead, Jesus commissions her to worship in the
Spirit and in truth. In other words, let God lead you in how
you live your life (the Spirit), and live your life acknowledging
the reality of who is leading it (truth). After her conversation
with Jesus, the woman went back to her town and told her
neighbors that she might have found the One they had all been
waiting for. She was satisfied by Jesus and thirsty for more of
him at the same time. Finally, a man who wouldn't disappoint.

There you have it—Jesus' longer-than-ten-minutes conversation. We know she did proclaim him to be the Messiah
and savior of the world (John 4:29). What we also know is
that the Samaritan woman left *understanding how her story
fits into his story* and *with a new appetite for God*, not man.
These are two outcomes that every meaningful conversation
has the potential to accomplish. First, let's look at how Jesus
initiated this heart-to-heart.

Second Star to the Right

How do we initiate conversations that matter? Hopefully,
by now, it's clear that relationships aren't formed so that we
can have a conversation about the gospel. At no point are we

required to give a clear presentation of the road to salvation. Instead, think of any relationship you have that you would consider meaningful. That relationship requires that you go deeper than sports or the weather. You have to discuss the things that get under your skin and those things that are close to your heart. A good talk with someone gets to the root of who they are and gives you insight into what is helping them grow. If the impression is right, your intentions are clear, and you're willing to invite them into your life, how about taking the step that Jesus took by asking them about something they are familiar with? For the Samaritan, it was water. For Ethan, it was Peter Pan.

One of the ways I have done this is by asking my friends which book has really shaped them. (If you're not a reader, then you must be listening to this through audiobook.) Try this same concept with movies. If you don't like books or movies, having conversations with people in the twenty-first century might just be a challenge.

Ethan told me his favorite book was *Peter and Wendy* by J. M. Barrie. He grew up in an all-boys school and was always fascinated with the idea of escaping to Neverland. He even had a tattoo to prove it.

Peter Pan . . . I thought to myself. *Isn't that a children's story?* Boy, was I wrong. The real story of Peter Pan is anything but a children's story.

"I would like to read a book that has had an impact on you, and then let's talk about it next time we get coffee," I told him. "After that you can read a book that has been impactful to me. Same thing." Our discussions went deep into what has developed the way we think, and then we politely challenged those thoughts.

From Neverland we went to the fantastical kingdom of Glome in C. S. Lewis's book *Till We Have Faces*. From Glome we traveled to Narnia. We stayed in Narnia for a bit to keep talking about whether Jesus and Aslan were actually alike. From Narnia we came back to earth, where Ethan realized heaven is a lot more to be desired than Neverland, and he can have Jesus now, while he is waiting. He didn't ever visit our church or any church, for that matter. What started with a question about something he is familiar with ended with the freedom to worship God in the Spirit and in truth as we walked around the lake.

Relationships with nonbelievers are like the rings of a tree, reopened with every emotional conversation. What has formed them? Which characters do they identify with, and why? Explain the insights you had while reading their favorite book or watching their favorite movie. If they feel like they have contributed to your growth, they will probably let you contribute to theirs. Worst-case scenario, you learn something you didn't know before. Best-case scenario, they find Someone they didn't have before.

Spicy Drinks

One of my many parenting fails was giving our (now) five-year-old, Brennan, a soda early on. The perfect mixture of carbonation and sugary syrup was an immediate hit with her. Brennan loves all types of sodas. Bring on the sweet fizz! When she was younger, however, she couldn't pronounce what she was tasting. And to her underdeveloped taste buds, carbonated drinks were best described as "spicy drinks." Technically, she called them "ficy drinks," but we were working on pronunciation. We have asked the girls if they want spicy drinks for so long now that we forget the waiter doesn't know what we are talking about. It's insider language that makes sense to us. Totally appropriate when we are talking to each other, but strange and misunderstood when outside the house.

Conversations are made up of words, and words are pointless if they don't make sense to both parties. To show the Samaritan woman that her story fits into God's bigger story, Jesus used language that she understood. Drinking water was an illustration that made sense to her. When we initiate conversations with people who don't think like us, we need to be aware that they may or may not know what we are talking about. We might be dealing with the same vocabulary but a different dictionary.

Make sure that your illustrations make sense, and that your words aren't insider language. Paul quoted the poets in Athens, while Peter quoted the prophet Joel in Jerusalem. Both were speaking of the same God. Even more, both were speaking with the same authority. God wasn't more glorified because Peter quoted directly from Joel. God was equally glorified because the listeners understood what they were saying and the conversation continued.

Words like *sin*, *testimony*, *blood of the Lamb*, and *infallibility* may not land well on unbelieving ears. Instead, try defining the terms you are tempted to use. Here is an example:

- *Insider language*: "Tomorrow I get to share my testimony with our church."
- *Universal language*: "Tomorrow I get to talk with some new friends about how far I've come in life."

We shouldn't be offended that we have to change the language we use based on who we are around. If I find myself talking to an accountant, I'm grateful that they adapt their insider language to be sensible to laypeople like me. If I want to teach my children about paying off debt, I can't pull out a mortgage-loan calculator. They need to do chores to pay off the toy we purchased for them before they play with it. "When I was a child, I talked like a child, I thought like a child, I reasoned like a child. When I became a man, I put the ways of childhood behind me" (1 Corinthians 13:11, NIV). Talk about spiritual things in a way that makes sense to them. It's not a compromise if you do; it's a compromise if you don't!

Nine-year-old Laurence was an eager fan of *The Chronicles of Narnia*. So much so, he admitted that he may love the Christ-figure, Aslan, more than Christ himself. Concerned, his mother wrote C. S. Lewis to find out what she should do. Lewis responded with the following:

Tell Laurence from me, with my love . . . [He] can't *really* love Aslan more than Jesus, even if he feels that's what he is doing. For the things he loves Aslan for doing or saying are simply the things Jesus really did and said. So that when Laurence thinks he is loving Aslan, he is really loving Jesus: and perhaps loving Him more than he ever did before. . . . I don't think he *need* be bothered at all. God knows all about the way a little boy's imagination works (He made it, after all).[3]

What Now?

How should our conversations end? It seems insincere to tell people I'll be praying for them every time they share their troubles. An invitation to church is hardly an invitation to another conversation. At the same time, I'm not a fan of "See you when I see you." Those are the worst! Intentionally initiating conversations that matter feel turbulent if we don't know where we are going or how to land the plane when we get there.

In the old paradigm of street preachers and tent revivals, it was all about how you close the deal to make a convert. In the even older paradigm of Jesus and the Samaritan woman, it was about creating a craving. One feels forceful, while the other feels inspiring. God's desire is for us to crave him more than anything. Quite honestly, the last thing this world needs is for me to create a convert who thinks, looks, and acts like me. White, theologically minded males with beards and thick-rimmed glasses are hardly in short supply. The world needs an appetite for God, one hungry sinner at a time.

Cravings start when someone has been teased with a taste of something they can't fully enjoy at the time. A kiss from my wife on my way out the door. A FaceTime call with my kids when I'm away traveling. A Sam's Club sample around 2:00 p.m. While in this life, none of us will be able to fully enjoy God. Every experience of him is a tease of what is to come. It creates the craving. I'm envious of the disciples for this very reason. They got to be with God without being with God forever. The closest any of us will ever get to heaven on earth. So for the time being, let's all try to be like Jesus to others by pointing out the hope that is here now and the hope that will eventually be here forever.

"A time is coming and has now come," Jesus told the woman. We have to say the same thing in different ways. We extend the presence of God to people when we are able to show hope in their situation. It shouldn't be hard work if it is our perspective on life. Always setting our hearts on the hope we have in Christ, we see others' situations not as they see them. Unfaithful marriages are not doomed. Suicide attempts are not reoccurring. It takes faith to believe the reality that God is always among us.

Initiating conversations that matter is not so that we can create converts. It's so that we can taste the goodness of God with others, leaving us both craving more.

8

IMITATION

How to Redefine Progress

Coming together is a beginning, staying together is a progress,
and working together is success.

HENRY FORD

My father told me, "Don't ever miss a good chance to shut up."

DR. PHIL (AND DR. PHIL'S DAD)

I WAS DEVASTATED. The first baptism at our church plant, and not one person from the Doubters' Club was in the tank. It was no secret that my hopes were high for the atheist co-moderator who started the club with me. I imagined it taking place like a domino effect. He would emerge from the horse trough (we were a church plant) hands in the air, everyone cheering, and before the end of service, his girlfriend would follow suit. Then his mom. Then possibly the two agnostic baristas making pour-overs for every person attending service. After them, the skeptic from down the street who attended the church since its first public gathering. His fiancée, Sophie, would follow him to the front if she saw what was going on. Sophie was one of the greeters. Her smile would fool anyone into thinking she was the most saved person in the building. I imagined the line getting longer and longer. From Sophie to Zack. Zack to Michelle. If Michelle would have brought her wife, maybe she would have joined in. All of this was merely aspirational, though. The Sunday of our first baptism, none of my friends from the Doubters' Club were in line. A few of them were watching. Most of them were busy serving.

And then it hit me . . . most of them were busy serving.

None of them had made Jesus their Savior, but all of them were on board with his mission. Is it possible that a person's behavior can mimic the person of Jesus even if they don't believe he is God?

Baptism is usually the goal when it comes to leading a person to Christ. Jesus was clear on this point: "Therefore go and make disciples of all nations, baptizing them in the name of the Father and of the Son and of the Holy Spirit, and teaching them to obey everything I have commanded you. And surely I am with you always, to the very end of the age" (Matthew 28:19-20, NIV). Baptism is the bat signal that a decision has been made to follow Jesus. If you believe in Jesus but haven't been baptized, it's your next step.

But what if you don't believe in Jesus?

In that case, I believe we should emphasize a different facet of Christianity. Not a highly intellectual, apologetics approach to finding truth, although this is appropriate in its time. Instead, perhaps you would want to try on a practical, change-the-world brand of Christianity. The hands and feet can be tender where the mouth has been irritating. More and more, my interactions with skeptics are reassuring me that convincing people they are wrong is not as transformative as letting them contribute to making things right. In *The Lord of the Rings*, Éowyn makes a famous declaration after accepting life over death. "I will be a healer, and love all things that grow and are not barren," she says.[1] I believe that's what all of us want, believer or not.

If someone believes in Christ, they should get baptized. If they are not a believer, invite them to imitate Christ with you. Imitation, not immersion, is your next step with the unbeliever.

Invitations, Not Commandments

Commandments are reserved for those who have been baptized: "baptizing them in the name of the Father and of the Son and of the Holy Spirit, and teaching them to obey everything I have *commanded* you" (emphasis added). They are the marching orders for the soldier who has taken an oath. "If you love me," Jesus said, "you will obey my commands" (John 14:15, NCV). Consequently, we should have no expectation that people who don't believe in Jesus would ever feel an obligation to act like him. That does not mean, however, that they would not accept the invitation to his mission if it were ever extended.

Since they are not at a place to obey his commands, what about inviting them into the ways of Jesus? The mission. The purpose. The undertaking to change the world by renewing one community at a time. The cause of justice and love. Food for the hungry. Taking care of the widows and orphans. Making meals for homeless shelters and youth drop-in centers. It's a unique way of constantly keeping Jesus in front of them.

"What you do unto the least of these," he told his disciples, "you do unto me" (Matthew 25:40, author's paraphrase). Inviting people to help the least of these means they will see Jesus in a way they may never have seen him before. As the Suffering Servant. Not the highly exalted, unreachable, polished Jew who deserves praise and demands surrender on Sunday mornings. Those of us who know him welcome that sort of Jesus because we know him as Savior. But before we knew him as Savior, we met him as Suffering Servant. For our sake. Thus, the crucified King is the One that we came to know and love. And we are reminded of the suffering Christ every time we help the ones who are suffering.

For our doubting brothers and sisters, the suffering of the world has been an indicator that an all-knowing, all-powerful God could not possibly exist. If God knows about all the stray bullets but chooses not to stop them, surely he couldn't be "good." The problem of pain and suffering in the world has been called the "rock of atheism." As long as I can remember, we have been doing everything we can to move that rock for the skeptic. I say, let them stub their toes. Trip over the rock, if that's what it takes. Let's come face-to-face with the pain in the world until we put our efforts toward resolving it. Not cognitively rationalizing its existence. If that could work, it would have worked by now. Suffering is where we find Jesus, not where we find out about him. The Doubters' Club has been a great place to stimulate the mind around this topic, but at some point, Jesus has to walk down the long staircase between the head and heart.

That's when helping those who are in need comes in. Being with the less fortunate has a way of softening our hearts. It takes the attention off of us and puts it on another. And this tests all our deepest-held convictions. If it is survival of the fittest, why do we have the impulse to inconvenience ourselves for the least of these? Wouldn't it be a better use of our temporal existence to make the most of every moment for our sake? Or at least for the sake of our kin, since they would be our only way of outlasting this life? And all this subconscious reasoning is interrupted by the cough of a child with cancer. Or the sockless feet of a homeless teen. Somehow, Jesus is there in that room. Interrupting thoughts and softening hearts. By helping those in need, we are, in the most practical sense, preparing our hearts for the King to enter. I think this is why people must join the mission. It awakens their heart to the need of a Savior, and it softens their heart to receive him.

Behind the Counter

It's common to hear the phrase "belong before you believe." The idea is that people need to experience a sense of belonging before they will believe the fundamental truths of who Jesus is. For the most part, I agree. I just think that, in an attempt to have a memorable phrase, we haven't fully captured what gives someone a sense of belonging. Belonging comes from participating. It comes from contributing to a cause. We know this from ordinary tasks like baking a cake. I belong in the kitchen when I'm stirring the batter. My wife will tell me to get out of the kitchen if I just keep tasting the bowl. And when the timer goes off, if I was part of making the cake, I have every right to call it my cake. I might have a slice myself, but not without sharing it. "Look what I helped make," I would tell the others around the table. Over time, I might even become a disciple of cake making. All because I contributed instead of just consumed.

In the Doubters' Club training, we call this the "behind the counter" moment. There was a moment when a barista at my favorite coffee shop invited me behind the counter to try and make a latte myself. Up until that point, I was an interested spectator, and sometimes consumer, of their lattes. Always intrigued by the way they whipped the foam into a tulip or swan. The espresso beans were interesting, too. The reason they grind the beans right before the shot goes into the drink is because beans should be used within fifteen minutes of being ground. Otherwise, you lose the defining notes of that particular bean. Months of learning from random conversations, and then the invitation.

"Preston, would you like to come behind the counter and try it yourself?"

I looked behind me to see a line of people waiting to order. They laughed and motioned for me to take her up on the offer. I didn't know what I was doing. I was sure to make a mess of their drinks. Latte art was absolutely off the table.

"Go for it!" One of the customers exclaimed.

I laughed with every order, knowing it was going to be an epic fail. A latte failures, to be exact. To my surprise, nobody was frustrated. Whether out of courtesy or sheer luck on my part, I don't even remember anyone returning their drink. It only lasted for a few moments, but I left that experience with a new appreciation for all things coffee. Later that day, I searched Amazon for an affordable version of the 220-volt Astra MEGA III. (That's an espresso machine, in case you didn't know.) My interest in coffee beans became an obsession the moment she invited me behind the counter.

Have you ever had that moment with a nonbeliever? The moment you invite them to participate in the Jesus you talk about all the time? Chances are high that they would give it a shot. I bet they would give financially to the widow on your street. They probably have a special interest in the local elementary school. Have you asked them to help you find a way to renovate the cafeteria? What causes are you part of as a direct result of your love for Jesus? Invite them behind the counter. Their outlook on Jesus might change if they have a chance to be like him.

Habits, Affections, and Stories

Whether you heard it in a counselor's office or read it in a spiritual-formation book, you probably know that it's common to revisit the stories in our lives if we want to change our habits. We show up in the world in a certain way based on how we interpret stories from our past. A girl who was told to never leave the house without makeup on might interpret that event as the moment she was told that she is not beautiful. Twenty years later, it's likely that she is self-conscious. Especially without any makeup. This is a type of cognitive behavioral therapy (CBT) that has been demonstrated effective with drug addiction, depression, anxiety, and a wide variety of mental illnesses. This is the strategy author Gregory Boyd uses in his book *Escaping the Matrix*. Referring to our false selves as "the matrix," Boyd writes: "We can think of the Matrix as the total web of lies we've internalized that keep us living in contradiction to our true self—the self that is defined by God through Christ alone."[2]

The lies we tell ourselves are deeply personal, and they extend far into our past. They are formed by the way we interpret our experiences, and those experiences have the strongest influence on how we act. Before our stories form habits, they develop affections in our lives. Affections are feelings of fondness that we have about a certain thing. Take the girl who thinks she needs to wear makeup as an example. She might develop an affection for Instagram models who show off lipstick, mascara, or foundation. It could be where a lot of her money goes, as well. Obviously, seeing all those models everyday would develop some habits. Stories create affections, and affections create habits. Here's why that matters.

Doubters have a habit of resisting the Christian faith. We don't have to speculate. By and large, stories from their past have created an affection for deconstructing doctrines. Much of this is done as a defense mechanism to help cope with reliving the story that led to the habit. For example, one of my atheist friends prayed for his sick sister when he was seven. His sister had cancer, and he prayed that God would heal her. After months of prayer, they had to amputate his sister's leg so the cancer didn't grow. My friend interpreted that event as God not answering his prayers. Therefore, God doesn't answer prayers. It would be an almost impossible task to think we could drill down to the formative story of why people think the way they do. We can help them experience new stories, however.

That will form new affections.

And form new habits.

We have attempted spiritual formation backward in the past. Help them get it right, teach them about devotion to Christ, and then watch their story change. I'd venture to say that the main distinction between an unsaved and a saved person would typically boil down to their habits. You can help people participate in the story of God. Show them how their story weaves into God's story by inviting them to imitate Christ with you through the way you are bringing healing to the community. In the Doubters' Club, we have seen time and again when unbelievers' affections for Christ are stirred because they have been participating in the mission. And you guessed it: Then their habits start to change. Back to a verse I quoted earlier in this chapter: "If you love me, show it by doing what I've told you" (John 14:15, MSG).

You can count it as progress when your unbelieving friend joins into the story of God. From there, affections will stir, and habits will form.

Heart of Stone

The downtown Denver Doubters' Club location was getting too big to maintain its integrity as a dialogical setting. People would come to a meeting and never get a chance to speak. I invited my friend, Drew, to lead a separate location with one of the Christians who was also attending. Drew taught me that atheists can be more vulnerable than Christians in a short amount of time. He held his heart on his sleeve in the most appropriate way. He was a good friend who loved well. I knew he would do a great job co-moderating a Doubters' Club. I felt Jesus was asking me to multiply the Doubters' Club, so I invited him into the mission. He kindly said, "H*** yea! I'm in. Let's have a drink and talk details."

Their club went as smoothly as would be expected with two gentle, fun-loving personalities leading the crew. In addition to their monthly meeting, Drew would attend our church. I never asked why, but I always assumed it was because he had formed such a strong relationship with the people in our faith community. Our church met on Sunday nights, and after every service, he was eager to keep the night going. I couldn't keep up with all the invitations to late-night movies and appetizers. As a rule of thumb, I would say no unless my family could come. After a long day of setup and teardown, it was important that my girls knew they took priority. But one night, I made an exception.

I was walking to the lobby to greet everyone on their way out when I was stopped by Drew. With tears in his eyes, he asked, "Can we talk? I know there are a lot of people here, but I need to talk about something you said." Drew always sat in the back. No one else heard the unsteadiness in his voice.

"Sure. Let's go to the café area." The order of service was such that most of our worship was at the end of the program. Our hopes were that this would allow time for affections to be stirred by the gospel story. This was certainly the case for Drew.

"At the end of the message, you shared a story about Aslan breathing on stone statues." Drew remembered it quite well. "When you told that story, I felt something happen inside my heart. I still feel deeply moved. I feel like someone was breathing on my heart."

The story I shared was from C. S. Lewis's *The Lion, the Witch and the Wardrobe*. Susan and Lucy were with Aslan as he approached all the statues in the witch's courtyard. The statues were loyal Narnians who had refused to join the White Witch. The part of the story I shared was the following:

The courtyard looked no longer like a museum; it looked more like a zoo. Creatures were running after Aslan and dancing round him till he was almost hidden in the crowd. Instead of all that deadly white the courtyard was now a blaze of colors. . . . And instead of the deadly silence the whole place rang with the sound of happy roarings, brayings, yelpings, barkings, squealings, cooings, neighings, stampings, shouts, hurrahs, songs and laughter.[3]

Drew identified with the statues. And all the outreaches he was helping with, all the Doubters' Club meetings, they all were like the breath of God on his heart. Softened for this moment, he asked if I would be willing to grab a bite with him to talk about what's going on.

"Of course," I said. "Let's hurry before anyone sees you crying." We both laughed. We both cried. We both shared our affections for Jesus.

Want to Be a Zookeeper?

Why is the most cause-oriented generation not connecting with the most cause-oriented organization in the world? We must invite people to participate in imitating Christ with us! If you are already participating in a mission that unbelievers would join, keep going! Extend the invitation. Make them feel empowered by your friendship and inspired by why you do the mission. Trust the process. If you aren't participating in a mission that would feel like common ground with an unbeliever, I invite you to consider starting a Doubters' Club.

In the history of the organization, we have never had an atheist or agnostic tell us that they don't want to help with the mission. We will train you to make sure that you start a healthy club in your community. By doing so, you will be inviting many people into a new story that God desires to write.

His pen is ready.

All he needs is a willing Jesus follower who longs to have conversations with non-Jesus followers. Visit thedoubtersclub.com to get trained. The Doubters' Club is proof that sometimes behavior imitates faith before the mind does.

9

CONCLUDING
WITH THE CLIFFSNOTES

How to Get This Party Started!

You gotta fight for your right to party.
BEASTIE BOYS

Anything not saved will be lost.
NINTENDO WII'S "QUIT SCREEN" MESSAGE

IN 2019, a study from the Barna Group revealed that Christians are backing away from evangelism. Almost half of those surveyed who were born between 1980 and 2000 said that it is wrong for them to share their faith. Not just socially painful. Morally wrong. To put it in their own words, "It is wrong to share one's personal beliefs with someone of a different faith in hopes that they will one day share the same faith."[1] I wasn't among the thousands who were interviewed, but had I been, I would have agreed. Sharing my beliefs in order to convert someone feels shallow. Unimpressive. Disingenuous. Don't misunderstand what I am saying, I do want people to find and follow Jesus. My disagreement is not with the "sharing my beliefs" part. My disagreement is with the "someone" part.

Someone.

Who?

A random someone?

Because the someones I know have names, and I don't call them "someones." I call them neighbors, coworkers, and in the best-case scenarios, friends. Actually, I don't call them friends. I call them by their name. That unique identifier that reassures them that they are the center of my attention for the moment. Dale Carnegie believed that a person's name is the sweetest sound they can hear.[2] Think about the last time someone used your name. Did it sound sweeter than normal? Was the interaction more memorable? Did you get, as Brennan Manning writes, "an extended case of the happies"?[3] There is a giant difference between when my neighbor says, "Good morning!" and when they say, "Good morning, Preston!" One puts the emphasis on the morning. The other puts the emphasis on me. Names are powerful! The use of a name directs all the energy of a compliment or statement into one individual. We become the center of the world when our names are used.

Statements become wildly personal.

Questions become fascinating journeys.

Compliments become courageous gestures of kindness.

And yes, that even means insults can become toxins running through our minds as we replay the hurt. The power of life and death is truly in the tongue. Greater life when your name is tagged on. Greater death too. I don't know about you, but I accept the risk. I accept the risk of being deeply hurt because my neighbor knows my name, as opposed to being a nameless someone. Every someone has a name worth knowing.

Evangelism without relationship has its place. Rarely is that place with the skeptic. The skeptic has individual hesitations about the faith. There is a personal reason they are resistant to Christianity. Without their name, we will never know that story. Without that story, friendship with Jesus has no chance. Story wraps flesh around the someones. As long as skeptics merely remain "someones," the best we can do is give them the CliffsNotes of the Jesus story, while getting the abbreviated version of theirs. The shortened version of what is most important to you meets the shortened version of what is most important to them. And so it goes. As long as skeptics remain someones to us, we will remain fools to them as we tell an abridged version of the greatest story in the history of mankind! I'm convinced that it's the CliffsNotes of Christianity that sound like a fairy tale, not Christianity itself.

This is the case, mainly, because fairy tales are written about something that happened in the past. From "once upon a time" to "happily ever after," all before bedtime. The CliffsNotes of Christianity are told in such a form. If we are not careful, we breeze through the powerful Good News like it was something that happened instead of something that *is happening*. That is not compelling enough for the skeptic. Rational minds demand reality in real time—which is exactly what Jesus plans on giving them.

Instead of CliffsNotes Christianity, what if you lived a go-to-the-edge-of-the-cliff Christianity? A Christianity that believes Jesus is currently waiting to throw a dinner party with the doubters, but he won't do it until all the guests are present.

Any guesses where the soon-to-be guests live?

On the Edge of the Cliff

In this journey we're setting out on, we cannot forget the story of the cliff dwellers. It's written by Luke, a disciple who must have known what it was like to be an analytical outsider. Luke was an evidence-based author who, like many of us, found himself more skeptical than the average Jew. The only Gentile in an all-Jewish cast of New Testament authors, Luke ends up being the most vigorous champion of the "someones" that have no name. He breaks social norms by making women, common laborers like shepherds, and the racially diverse the heroes. Oftentimes, Luke records Jesus telling his disciples about the importance of pursuing a life-transforming relationship with the outsider. Luke 15 is the most famous example, with the parables of the lost sheep, lost coin, and prodigal son. But it's what Luke wrote in the less-famous chapter 14 that I find particularly instructive on this matter: the parable of the cliff dwellers. It's where Jesus untangles the myth of comfortable evangelism. A story that illustrates how life with God cannot be reduced to conversion in a temple. Life with God is an invitation to a table.

Imagine the scene taking place. Everyone is about to start eating when Jesus notices how the people at the table are elbowing their way to the best seat (something my children do when they don't want to sit next to each other). Just before telling them about the cliffs, he calls them out on their childish behavior. Eugene Peterson paraphrases Jesus' interaction here perfectly: "What I'm saying is, If you walk around all high and mighty, you're going to end up flat on your face. But if you're content to be simply yourself, you will become more than yourself" (Luke 14:11, MSG). There isn't time for an elitist game of musical chairs. "Don't try to act like you're better than you are," Jesus is telling them. "The only one in the room worthy of honor is the host, and the host wants to sit next to the doubters. Where are the doubters?" Taking a sip from his cup, Jesus tells the following story.

A man once gave a great banquet and invited many. And at the time for the banquet he sent his servant to say to those who had been invited, "Come, for everything is now ready." But they all alike began to make excuses. . . . So the servant came and reported these things to his master. Then the master of the house became angry and said to his servant, "Go out quickly to the streets and lanes of the city. . . ."

And the servant said, "Sir, what you commanded has been done, and still there is room." And the master said to the servant, "Go out to the highways and hedges and compel people to come in, that my house may be filled."

LUKE 14:16-18, 21-23

After those who had been invited to the banquet refused to attend, the servant is told to go into the streets—find the people who are likely to accept the invitation. Most likely, these would be the spiritual seekers of their day. The C-E-O churchgoers of ours. Christmas and Easter Only. Interested in faith but not devoted to God.

"We did that, and there are still open seats. Should we move to a smaller table?"

"No!" the Host exclaims. "My house has big tables for a reason. The more the merrier. Go past the city limits. Go to the countryside. Wait! Follow the highways all the way to the cliffs. Go to the cliffs! I know the people at the cliffs are as far away from this place as possible, but compel them to join us. We aren't starting the party until everyone is here."

All those who were listening to Jesus knew something about the highways and hedges. No one lived on the highways and hedges; those were paths that led you through the countryside. And the countryside ended at the cliffs. That's where Jesus' temptation took place, and that's where he cast a legion of demons into pigs. The God haters of the day were at the cliffs. They were the ones most disinterested in life with God—just like God haters from our own time. The party might be on hold for a while if we have to wait for the people on the edge of the cliff: the doubters. The skeptics. The deeply hurt. The son. The daughter. The mother. The father. The one you have been thinking about throughout this whole book. Jesus holds ground for them by delaying the party. Even if all your attempts to convert them have failed, Jesus still has hope. The Host tells the servant to "compel" the cliff dwellers. He never said to convert them.

Living a Compelling Life

In full disclosure, the word *compel* has been exploited in the past. After Constantine converted to Christianity, he became crazy with his newfound faith and nationalized it. That is, he persecuted anyone who wasn't Christian, forcing them to become a Christian who thought and acted as he did. And he used this verse from Luke 14 to justify it. He would quote this verse and say that he was "compelling" people to follow Jesus. The Spanish Inquisition did the same thing. In the late 1400s, people from the Islamic or Jewish faith were compelled to become Christians—compelled to confess Christ or otherwise be tortured, lose their possessions, or die.[4] Many of my Doubters' Club friends know this word in the same way. Exegete it how we will, they have experienced what it means for their parents or other loved ones to "compel" them back to church. If we don't know this, we will end up whistling in a graveyard that we helped populate.

Notice the Host doesn't send out soldiers; he sends out a servant. Servants compel in a very different way. The context of the word *compel* used here is best understood as insistent hospitality for an extended period. What a relief! You are in it for the long haul. The Host—Jesus—said so. We haven't failed because our friends don't share our same beliefs. We are doing exactly what Jesus asked us to do if we are helpful, hopeful, and kindhearted. Always inviting them into his story but never taking it personally when they don't choose to join. Unfortunately, some of them will never choose to join.

You have heard a lot of stories about people who have ended up following Jesus through the Doubters' Club. In all reality, there are far more who are still living on the edge. I don't know if they will ever come home. Sometimes we are faced with the troubling reality that certain people will never choose to follow Jesus. Holding on to Christian clichés about perseverance and deathbed salvations only complicates things. It puts too much pressure on both parties. And the disappointment is almost unbearable. The awful truth is that not everyone will end up with God forever. Some of the seats will be empty when it's time for dinner. So, what should we do?

Live a compelling life! You may be uncertain about whether or not your unbelieving friends are going to be at the marriage supper of the Lamb, but invite them to your table. Let them experience what true, Christlike hospitality looks like. Don't give up on them. Make spending time with you so incredible that they never want it to end. Time at your table is just a mere shadow of the true fellowship they could have forever with the Creator.

Listen to their story (chapters 1–3).

Look for the questions (chapters 4–6).

And learn with them (chapters 7–8).

My barber and I were having a normal conversation about life, politics, and the Doubters' Club. "You know what I love most about the Doubters' Club?" he said. "Ever since I became an atheist, I have really missed the community that I used to find at church. The Doubters' Club is that community for me. And we are learning together. I like having friends who are willing to listen to, and learn from, one another." You can create this sort of community as well! Whether you start a Doubters' Club or host the next Thanksgiving meal at your place, why not use the table as a sort of hospital for doubters? A hospital for those skeptics who run, full pace, away from the church. Who have fallen off the cliff. What a surprise it would be to them to find hospitals at the bottom of the cliffs! A group of wounded healers who refuse to give up until the seats are full.

Catch Them on the First Bounce

In *Everybody, Always*, author Bob Goff wrote about an experience he had while attending a skydiving class. As he listened to the basic dos and don'ts of deploying your parachute, the instructor went on to describe what happens if someone hits the ground without one. "Hitting the ground isn't what kills you. Every bone in your body will break, of course. But after you hit the ground, you'll bounce—and it's the second time you hit that kills you as the broken bones puncture all your organs."[5] Albeit a morbid illustration, the point is also true of disciple-making. Continuing the analogy of Luke 14, unbelievers are running off the cliff at an unprecedented rate. Some of them are cliff dwellers, but more and more are becoming cliff jumpers. It is still possible to catch them on the first bounce.

You can do it! You can turn any table into a hospital by giving the doubter space, time, and the listening ear they need. In this, you will show them Christ's Kingdom. A Kingdom of theological misfits, cliff jumpers, ex-churchgoers, and double-minded doubters. A Kingdom that looks more like a clinic at the bottom of the cliff. Every clinic needs practitioners, and you have been recruited. You get to be the medic who gives the individual care required for doubters to recover. You get to be the brain surgeon who opens their minds to new truths. You get to be the chiropractor who realigns the crooked soul trying to stand up straight. You need no formal training or credentials to be used in these ways. "I came to serve, and not be served," Jesus said. Quickly followed by, "and you cannot be greater than your Master" (Matthew 20:26-28; Mark 10:43-45; John 13:12-16; author's paraphrase). When you are serving the cliff jumpers, you are as great as you will ever be.

As you embark on the courageous journey of intentionally befriending atheists and skeptics, remember that your way of living is tethered to authors and concepts far older than this book. You are reorienting people to a Jesus-looking-God by adopting a center set mindset (see pages 20–21). You are instrumental in probing spiritual curiosity with those on the negative side of the Engel Scale as they move toward trusting God (see pages 51–52). And if you go back far enough, you are participating in the mission of Jesus by simply seeking those who are lost.

So start a Doubters' Club. Start a new conversation with your neighbor. Start another pot of coffee with your unbelieving friend. These are your hospital scrubs for the day. If all they end up doing is talking about the emotional and intellectual damage that has been done to them by the church, good. That means you caught them on the first bounce. Use this book as your bedside manner. Don't forget that every conversion story is different. Don't forget the Five *I*s. And most importantly, don't give up on the doubter! As long as they are with you, they are experiencing the healing love of Christ. Your greatest chance at making their life about Jesus is by making your life about them.

ACKNOWLEDGMENTS

First, I would like to thank my literary agent, Greg Johnson, who believed in this book years before I ever typed a sentence . . . and who wouldn't let the idea go! Greg met with me when the Doubters' Club was just a small gathering, and he asked me to write a book. Over two years later, I finally emailed him that I was totally in. His enthusiasm for this project has never wavered! The field of publishing will never be the same because Greg has believed in so many first-time authors like myself.

Thank you to NavPress and their entire leadership team. I'm unbelievably grateful for the commitment they have had to seeing this book influence as many lives as possible. Specifically, my editor David Zimmerman. David has a levity to his emails and interactions that helps me breathe deep around every deadline. And thank you, Elizabeth Schroll, for being the most impressive copy editor I have ever met. David and Elizabeth are the secret weapons behind this book. They brought precision to every page, while making it flow seamlessly for you, the reader. I always reread their compliments to me. It always means so much coming from the professionals.

A big shout-out to the team at Tyndale! Their entire team sets the standard for prompt responses and excellence. Julie Chen did the cover work for the book, and I could not have been more pleased! A tremendous amount of thought went into those three stacked cups. She saw what even I couldn't see, and I'm grateful for that. I intentionally stack coffee cups when doing the dishes, just to remind me that life isn't perfect and messes can be beautiful. Well done, Julie Chen and Whitney Harrison!

I would also like to thank Mom and Dad—two people who taught me to be inquisitive as a child and made room for Jesus in our home. I love you both dearly. I wouldn't know Jesus without you!

A special thanks must also be made to Jeff Magruder. He was my "detour guide" when I walked away from traditional Christianity. I'm a Christian thinker because of him.

To all those original Doubters' Club participants—Trax, Andrew, Jon, and Alex, just to mention a few. They taught me that questions can be more satisfying than answers.

There are so many other individuals and organizations that have made this book a reality. I owe a tremendous debt of gratitude to two pastors, Scott Wilson and Jeremy Johnson. Scott has shaped my soul to hear from God and to never stop moving forward in life. Jeremy has championed this book and its ideas from the first time we met. Plus, some of the one-liners in this book are from our lunch and coffee meetings. Steve Pike taught me everything I know about preconversion discipleship, and he is someone I will always learn from. My spiritual SEAL team—Andy Lehmann, Allen Kendrick, and Shawn Ulmer. You all are my guardrails in life.

At the risk of sounding cheesy, I want to thank the entire Church Multiplication Network (CMN) team of directors—John Davidson, John Jay Wilson, Mike McCrary, Jeffery Portmann, and Chris Railey. CMN allowed me the space and encouragement I needed to see this book through. Each one of them has mentored me, and I have no plans for putting an end to my annoying questions about church and discipleship. Thank you to my assistant, Emilie Lamb, for taking so much off my calendar so that the message of the Doubters' Club can spread. You are a rock star!

And most importantly, I would like to thank my wife, Lisa, and our two daughters, Piper Joy and Brennan Kay. Lisa has been this book's number-one fan from before it was even an idea. She stayed by my side when I was walking through my unbelief without judging me for thinking differently. I love how we are growing together in the Kingdom. And to my daughters, without whom this book would have been done much earlier, but it would have been incomplete. My girls are mentioned numerous times throughout the book because they remind this doubting soul of God's goodness and faithfulness. My end goal in life is to love people like my daughters do.

NOTES

INTRODUCTION: GREAT MINDS DO NOT THINK ALIKE

1. *Dictionary of Proverbs* (Hertfordshire, England: Wordsworth Editions, 2006), s.v. "Great wits jump."
2. Eric Hoffer, *Reflections on the Human Condition* (New York: Harper & Row, 1973), 55.
3. Flannery O'Connor, *The Complete Stories* (New York: Farrar, Straus and Giroux, 1971), 508.
4. This is the tag line for Boyd's ministry; see rcknew.org.

CHAPTER 1: GOD OF THE DOUBTER

1. Paul A. Djupe and Ryan P. Burge, "The Decline of Religion Continues—Nones Gain 3 Percent in One Year," *Religion in Public* (blog), October 7, 2020, https://religioninpublic.blog/2020/10/07/the-decline-of-religion-continues-nones-gain-3-percent-in-one-year/.
2. John S. Dickerson, *The Great Evangelical Recession: 6 Factors That Will Crash the American Church . . . and How to Prepare* (Grand Rapids, MI: Baker Books, 2013), 61.
3. Albert Camus, *Lyrical and Critical Essays*, ed. by Philip Thody (New York: Vintage Books, 1970), 169.
4. C. S. Lewis, *Surprised by Joy: The Shape of My Early Life* (New York: HarperOne, 2017), 279.
5. Alan Hirsch and Michael Frost, *The Shaping of Things to Come: Innovation and Mission for the 21st-Century Church* (Grand Rapids, MI: Baker Books, 2013), 68.
6. Ibid., 68.
7. Dr. Thomas L. Constable, *Notes on Luke*, 2021 edition, accessed February 10, 2021, https://planobiblechapel.org/tcon/notes/pdf/luke.pdf.

CHAPTER 2: GOD, I'M TIRED OF THIS

1. *Baker's Evangelical Dictionary of Biblical Theology*, s.v. "Friend, Friendship," accessed February 11, 2021, https://www.studylight.org/dictionaries/eng/bed/f/friend-friendship.html.

2. Brennan Manning, *The Ragamuffin Gospel: Good News for the Bedraggled, Beat up, and Burnt-Out* (Colorado Springs: Multnomah, 2015), 168.

3. As quoted in Amanda Woods, "Dr. Fauci Says Americans Should Never Shake Hands Again Due to Coronavirus," *New York Post*, April 9, 2020, https://nypost.com/2020/04/09/dr-fauci-makes-plea-that-americans-never-shake-hands-again/.

CHAPTER 3: GOD OF THE DETOUR

1. Hafiz, "The Great Religions," in *The Gift: Poems by Hafiz, the Great Sufi Master*, trans. Daniel Ladinsky (New York: Penguin Compass, 1999), 177.

2. J. R. R. Tolkien, *The Fellowship of the Ring: Being the First Part of the Lord of the Rings* (London: HarperCollins, 2020), 171.

3. Robert Robinson, "Come Thou Fount of Every Blessing," 1758. Public domain.

4. James F. Engel and Hugo Wilbert Norton, *What's Gone Wrong with the Harvest?: A Communication Strategy for the Church and World Evangelization* (Grand Rapids, MI: Zondervan, 1975).

5. James F. Engel, *Contemporary Christian Communications: Its Theory and Practice* (Nashville: Thomas Nelson, 1979), 77–83.

6. John Mark Comer, *The Ruthless Elimination of Hurry* (Colorado Springs: Waterbrook, 2019), 19.

7. Abraham Joshua Heschel, *God in Search of Man: A Philosophy of Judaism* (New York: Farrar, Straus and Giroux, 1976), 3.

CHAPTER 4: IMPRESSION

1. Cynthia Ozick, *Trust: A Novel* (London: MacGibbon & Kee, 1967), 560.

2. Sreechinth C., *Jim Rohn's Success Tips for an Exceptional Living* (Los Angeles: UB Tech, 2018), 14.

3. "Poison Dart Frog," Rainforest Alliance, updated September 1, 2012, https://www.rainforest-alliance.org/species/poison-dart-frog.

4. "Poison Frog," San Diego Zoo, accessed February 11, 2021, https://animals.sandiegozoo.org/animals/poison-frog.

5. Greg Boyd, "Greg on Politics," *ReKnew* (blog), November 10, 2014, https://reknew.org/2014/11/greg-on-politics/.

6. Piet Hein, *Mist and Moonshine: Grooks V* (Oxford: Blackwell, 1973), 14.

7. Martin B. Copenhaver, *Jesus Is the Question: The 307 Questions Jesus Asked and the 3 He Answered* (Nashville: Abingdon Press, 2014), xviii. The two studies he references are John Dear, *The Questions of Jesus: Challenging Ourselves to Discover Life's Great Answers* (New York: Doubleday, 2004), xxii; and Eric Burtness, *Lenten Journey: Beyond Question* (Minneapolis: Augsburg Fortress, 2012), 9.

8. Sam Harris, *Letter to a Christian Nation* (New York City: Vantage Books, 2008), xi–xii.

9. A. W. Tozer, *Three Spiritual Classics in One Volume: Knowledge of the Holy, The Pursuit of God, and God's Pursuit of Man* (Chicago: Moody, 2018), 13.

10. N. T. Wright, *Revelation for Everyone* (London: SPCK, 2011), 173.

CHAPTER 5: INTENTION

1. William Barclay, *The Gospel of Matthew Volume I*, rev. ed. (Louisville, KY: John Knox Press, 1975), 277.

2. Ibid., 274.

3. Terrence Real, *I Don't Want to Talk About It: Overcoming the Secret Legacy of Male Depression* (New York City: Scribner, 1997), 23.

4. Ibid., 37.

5. Thomas Merton, *The Sign of Jonas* (New York: Harcourt Brace Jovanovich, 1981), 323.

6. *John Wesley's Sermons: An Anthology*, ed. Albert C. Outler and Richard P. Heitzenrater (Nashville: Abingdon Press, 1991), 206.

7. For a quick reference to this, see Oxford Reference, "Adolf Jülicher," accessed February 11, 2021, https://www.oxfordreference.com/view/10.1093/oi /authority.20110803100026765.

CHAPTER 6: INVITATION

1. Charles R. Swindoll, *The Grace Awakening: Believing in Grace Is One Thing. Living It Is Another* (Nashville: Thomas Nelson, 2010), 295.

2. In a letter to Don Giovanni Calabria dated August 10, 1948; as quoted in *The Quotable Lewis*, ed. Jerry Root and Wayne Martindale (Wheaton, IL: Tyndale, 1989), 579.

3. C. S. Lewis, *The C. S. Lewis Signature Classics* (New York: HarperOne, 2017), 518.

4. "The Relation of Dress to Art," in *The Artist as Critic: Critical Writings of Oscar Wilde*, ed. Richard Ellmann (Chicago: University of Chicago Press, 1982), 18.

5. Jessica Stillman, "Science Has Just Confirmed That If You're Not Outside Your Comfort Zone, You're Not Learning," Inc.com, August 14, 2018,

https://www.inc.com/jessica-stillman/want-to-learn-faster-make-your-life
-more-unpredictable.html?cid=cp01002quartz&fbclid=IwAR2v9DwewsM
WZADRajTnNPXNs6-0JVblZoqBigm2BoFaZuju08O5zhIlw6k.

6. Ephrat Livni, "A New Study from Yale Scientists Shows How Uncertainty
   Helps Us Learn," *Quartz* (blog), July 31, 2018, https://qz.com/1343503/a
   -new-study-from-yale-scientists-shows-how-uncertainty-helps-us-learn/.

7. Jessica Stillman, "You Should Spent 70 Percent of Your Time Doing Hard
   Things, Says This 5-Time Entrepreneur," Inc.com, July 19, 2018, https://
   www.inc.com/jessica-stillman/follow-70-percent-rule-to-maximize-learning
   -says-this-5x-entrepreneur.html.

8. As quoted in Alan Fadling, *An Unhurried Life: Following Jesus' Rhythms of
   Work and Rest* (Downers Grove, IL: InterVarsity Press, 2013), 8–9.

CHAPTER 7: INITIATION

1. Lin-Manuel Miranda, "Aaron Burr, Sir," *Hamilton* © 2016 Atlantic
   Records.

2. Pat McCloskey, "The Rift between Jews and Samaritans," Franciscan
   Media, accessed December 3, 2020, https://www.franciscanmedia.org
   /ask-a-franciscan/the-rift-between-jews-and-samaritans.

3. C. S. Lewis, *Letters to Children*, ed. Lyle W. Dorsett and Marjorie Lamp
   Mead (New York: Touchstone, 1995), 52–53.

CHAPTER 8: IMITATION

1. J. R. R. Tolkien, *The Return of the King: Lord of the Rings Part Three* (New
   York: Del Rey, 2012), 262.

2. Gregory A. Boyd and Al Larson, *Escaping the Matrix: Setting Your Mind
   Free to Experience Real Life in Christ* (Grand Rapids, MI: Baker Books,
   2005), 22.

3. C. S. Lewis, *The Lion, the Witch and the Wardrobe: A Story for Children*
   (New York: Macmillan, 1950), 137.

CHAPTER 9: CONCLUDING WITH THE CLIFFSNOTES

1. Barna Group, "Almost Half of Practicing Christian Millennials Say
   Evangelism Is Wrong," barna.com, February 5, 2019, https://www.barna
   .com/research/millennials-oppose-evangelism/.

2. In his 1936 bestseller, Carnegie wrote: "Remember that a person's name is
   to that person the sweetest and most important sound in any language."
   Dale Carnegie, *How to Win Friends and Influence People* (New York: Pocket
   Books, 2010), 79.

3. Brennan Manning with John Blase, *All Is Grace: A Ragamuffin Memoir* (Colorado Springs: David C Cook, 2011), 135.
4. History.com, "Inquisition," updated August 21, 2018, https://www.history .com/topics/religion/inquisition#section5. For additional study, see Everett Ferguson, *Church History Volume One: From Christ to Pre-Reformation: The Rise and Growth of the Church in Its Cultural, Intellectual, and Political Context* (Grand Rapids, MI: Zondervan, 2005).
5. Bob Goff, *Everybody, Always: Becoming Love in a World Full of Setbacks and Difficult People* (Nashville: Nelson Books, 2018), 56.